Foodi Multi-Cooker Cookbook For Beginners

550 Recipes

For busy people 2020 EDITION

BY

REBECCA PACE

DISCLAIMER

The information contained in this book is geared for educational and entertainment purposes only. Strenuous efforts have been made towards providing accurate, up to date and reliable complete information. The information in this book is true and complete to the best of our knowledge. Neither the publisher nor the author takes any responsibility for any possible consequences of reading or enjoying the recipes in this book. The author and publisher disclaim any liability in connection with the use of information contained in this book. Under no circumstance will any legal responsibility or blame be apportioned against the author or publisher for any reparation, damages, or monetary loss due to the information herein, either directly or indirectly.

Table of Contents

INTRODUCTION

Meaning of Ninja Foodi

This is a new trending kitchen appliance. It is a pressure cooker that crisps. Ninja has a 6.5qt pressure cooker along with a 4qt Cook & crisp basket for the Tender Crisp (this is an Air Fryer function). It is correct to say that the Ninja Foodi is an Air Fryer, a pressure cooker and a dehydrator. The appliance allows you to turn ingredients that are tough to become tender, juicy and full of flavor.

It cooks food as faster as you could expect. The Ninja Foodi is usually called and ultimate Air Fryer due to its crisping lid that is powerful. Ninja Foodi is a unit that uses super-heated steam to put moisture and flavor into your foods. The crisping lid releases hot air all around your food for a crispy result. The Ninja Foodi is a combination of 4 in 1 appliance which includes: A pressure cooker, dehydrator, slow cooker and air fryer.

Benefits of Using the Ninja Foodi:

There are lots of benefits you can get from using this appliance. The benefit that outweighs other appliances is that it does not require you to flip the fries over to the other side many times compared to other pressure cookers. You may only shake the fries on halfway to cooking time for a proper cooking. The benefits are shown below:

1. **Crispy Wings**

Start cooking your chicken or turkey wings even in haste with the pressure cooker mode. When the normal cooking is done, switch to the air fryer to get that hot air circulating all around the wings and gives you a crispy result. You can combine with any sauce of your choice for your dinner or as an appetizer.

2. **Baked Macaroni and Cheese**

This unit allows you to cook macaroni and cheese and gives you a crispy result. When you are done with the normal cooking, you can swap to the Air Fryer mode for that crispy golden-brown topping that you would get when baked.

3. **Scalloped Potatoes**

Everybody loves a eating creamy scalloped potatoes. The unit tenders your potatoes and then with the air fryer for a crispy result. Ninja Foodi allows you to cook all kinds of food unlike other units like air fryer or pressure cooker.

4. **Pressure cook and crisp**

Ninja Foodi enables you to pressure cook something and then make it crispy. This crispiness makes the chicken you cook not to require that you bring the chicken to the broiler. Everything can stay neat and nice.

Cooking things at once is very beneficial and helpful to Ninja Foodi users because it is not time-consuming cooking a healthy food with the unit. The parts are easy to clean and it has a large cooking capacity.

Function Keys of Your Ninja Foodi:

Ninja Foodi comes with many buttons for optimum operation of the unit which includes steam, slow cook, pressure cook, sear/sauté button, air crisp, broil, bake /roast and keep warm, buttons respectively. It also has buttons for temperature and time controls, start/stop button. The buttons and their functions are shown below:

1. **Pressure cook:**

This button helps you to cook your meal up to 4 hours using high or low pressure. As earlier said, it is possible to adjust the cooking time to 1-minute increment for 1 hour. When the time is up, you may increase the time to 5 minutes and begin to cook up to 4 hours. Hence you can make a whole lot of meals.

2. **Air Crisp:**

This function gives you an opportunity to adjust the temperature to either 300°F or 400°F and also adjust to increase the cooking time to 2 minutes for the highest cooking time of 1 hour. The air crisp button is used in cooking many dishes like chicken tenders, French fries etc. Pressure cooked food can be crisp using this button.

3. **Bake/Roast:**

This setting in the Ninja is good for making roasted meats and baked foods. For this function, the Ninja Foodi uses the air-frying lid. There is no problem if you set the cooking time to 1-minute increment for 1 hour. When the time is up, you may increase the time to 5 minutes and begin to cook up to 4 hours. After the hour mark, you can increase the time in five-minute increments and cook for up to four hours.

4. **Steam:**

It is possible to steam your veggies and other meals by putting the pressure lid on the Ninja Foodi with the sealing valve in the vent position.

5. **Slow cook:**

This button also makes use of the pressure lid with the sealing valve in the vent position. It is possible for you to slow cook low or slow cook high. The cooking time can also be adjusted to 15 minutes increment for up to 12 hours. It is advisable to use the slow cook mode when cooking meals like stews, soup or pot roasts.

6. **Sear/Sauté:**

This button on the Ninja Foodi does not make use of the lid. It only has a temperature setting of 5 different modes respectively. These includes: medium, medium-high, high, low or medium-low, setting. Foods can be browned after cooking or before cooking. The button can also be used to make different kinds of sauces, gravies. This button functions the same as you would sear or sauté using your stovetop.

Ninja Foodi Pressure Releasing Methods:

This process is ideal for stopping all cooking process in order to avoid the food getting burnt. Foods like corn or broccoli etc. are ideal for this pressure releasing. There are two types of pressure release namely: Quick and natural pressure release.

1. **How to do a Ninja Foodi Quick Release**

Immediately the cooking time is up, keep the venting knob on Venting Position to enable Ninja Foodi quickly release the pressure inside the pressure cooker. To release all the pressure, it normally takes some few minutes. Before you open the lid, wait until the valve drops.

2. **How to do a Ninja Foodi Natural Release**

Immediately the cooking time is up, you have to wait until the valve drops and the lid is opened. In order to make sure all the pressure is released before opening the lid, keep the venting knob on Venting Position. This particular pressure release technique normally takes about 10 – 25 minutes but it depends on the amount of food in your cooker. To do the 10 – 15 minutes pressure release, when the cooking time is up, wait 10 – 15 minutes before moving the Venting Knob from Sealing Position to Venting Position so as to enable the remaining pressure to be released. Do not fail to wait for the floating valve to drop before you open the lid.

Steps on How to Use Your Ninja Foodi:

This appliance is a very friendly and easy-to-use kitchen unit.

For Ninja Foodi pressure cooker:

1. Always put your foods in the inner pot of the Ninja Foodi or you put your food in the Air Fryer basket. This is basically good for meats.

2. Press the power on function.

3. Close lid in place. Do not put the one that is attached.

4. Set the top steam valve to seal position and press the pressure function.

5. Adjust the temperature to either high or low using the + or – buttons respectively.

6. Set the cooking time using the + or – buttons.

7. Press Start button.

8. The Ninja Foodi will take a little time to reach pressure and then will count the number of minutes until it reaches zero minute.

For Ninja Foodi Air Fryer:

1. Make use of the lid that is attached.

2. Place the Air Fryer cooking basket inside the Ninja Foodi inner pot.

3. Place your food inside the cooking basket.

4. Lock the attached lid and switch on the Ninja Foodi by pressing the button at the bottom.

5. Push the air crisp button.

6. Select the temperature you want to use by pressing the + and – buttons.

7. Set the cooking time by pressing the + and – buttons.

8. Select start button.

Useful Tips & Tricks for Using Your Ninja Foodi

It is pertinent to inquire to know how to properly use a new appliance you bought. Ninja Foodi come with 2 distinct lids. One is for the electric pressure cooker while the other one is for the Air Fryer lid. It is possible to use both lids in on food. Immediately the pressure cooker is done, remove the pressure cooker lid and put the Air Fryer lid. This helps to crisp your food. Every new kitchen appliance you get comes with an operational manual to guide you on the proper usage of the unit. Below are some few tips for the proper usage of your Ninja Foodi:

1. Whenever you want to spray cooking spray on the inner pot of your Ninja Foodi, do not use aerosol cooking spray.

2. Try to use the recommended amount of water or broth if you are using the pressure-cooking button. Wrong usage of water may not give you the desired result.

3. When you are not using your Ninja Foodi, unplug from any power source so as to avoid the appliance switch on by itself even when you did not press the power on button.

4. It is not advisable to use your Ninja Foodi on your stove top. This can easily damage the unit.

Ninja Foodi Troubleshooting Tips

Every electronic appliance sometimes has trouble shooting or shows a faulty message on the display. Below are some of the major trouble shooting or problems you could find on your Ninja Foodi.

1. My appliance is taking a long time to come to pressure. Why?

It is important to know how long it takes your Ninja Foodi to come to pressure. Base on a particular temperature you choose, cooking time may vary. Temperature of the cooking pot at the moment of cooking including the amount of ingredients also makes cooking time to vary. If the cooking time is taking a longer time than necessary, make sure your silicone ring is fully seated and flush against the lid, make sure the pressure lid is fully closed and set the pressure release valve to seal position.

2. Why is the cooking time counting slowly?

You have to make sure you set the time correctly. Check if you did not use hours instead of minutes. Note that the HH stands for hours while the MM stands for minutes on the display window respectively. You can increase or decrease the cooking time.

3. How do I know when the appliance is pressurizing?

When the appliance is building pressure, the rotating lights will display on the display window. When you are using steam or pressure mode, light will rotate on the display screen. It means the appliance is preheating. Immediately the preheating process finishes, the normal cooking time starts counting.

4. When I'm using the steam mode, my unit is bringing out a lot of steam.

During cooking, steam releasing on the pressure release valve is normal. It is advisable to allow the pressure release valve in the vent position for Steam, Slow Cook, and Sear or Sauté mode.

5. Why can't I take off the pressure lid?

The Ninja Foodi has to be depressurized before the pressure lid can be opened. This is one of the safety measures put by the manufacturer. In order to do a quick pressure release, set the pressure release valve to the vent position. Immediately the pressure is released completely, the lid will be ready to open.

6. Do I need to lose the pressure release valve?

The answer is yes. You have to loosen the pressure release valve. It helps to circulate pressure through some release of small amount of steam while cooking is done for the result to be excellent.

Ninja Foodi Frequently Asked Questions and Answers:

Question 1: Can I deep fry chicken with this appliance?

Answer: Yes, it is possible. You can cook a chicken in your Ninja Foodi. This is a new modern way of cooking that can tender your food and progress to crisping the food using hot air and give you a crispy result.

Question 2: Can I Take My Ninja Pot from the Refrigerator and Put directly in the appliance?

Answer: Yes, you can do it if your pot was in the refrigerator.

Question 3: Can the Pot enter under the Broiler or the Oven?

Answer: Yes. It is possible but you have to be extra careful while putting or taking the pot out from the Ninja Foodi. It is only the lid that you do not need to put under the oven or the broiler.

Question 4: Can the Baking or cooking pan enter under the oven?

Answer: Yes. It is very possible and good to put the cooking pan under the oven. You just need to be careful while inserting the pan.

Question 5: Can I use the buffet settings to cook?

Answer: NO. It is not advisable to do that because the buffet function is just to keep temperature that is above 140°F when the food has been cooked to 165°F.

Question 6: What is the meaning of One-pot Meal Cooking?

Answer: These are important family meal that could be ready within 30 minutes time. The one pot helps in a quick clean up.

Question 7: What differentiate model op301 from model op305?

Answer: Model OP305 has the Dehydrate button while model OP301 has no dehydrate button. That's the major difference.

Question 8: Can you can food with Ninja Foodi?

Answer: No, you will not be able to can food with this appliance. You can only do it if you have a pressure canner can.

Question 9: Why is the time beeper not beeping?

Answer: You can check the volume level.

Question 10: Can I put frozen pork loin in my Ninja Foodi?

Answer: Yes. It is possible to do that. Frozen foods can be cooked with this appliance.

Question 11: If the Ninja foodi displays water, what is the meaning?

Answer: It means that you need to put more water into the Ninja Foodi. If at a point of putting more water and the error still show up, contact the customer care on 877581-7375.

Question 12: Can meat and cheese vegetables be cooked with this appliance?

Answer: No. Ninja Foodi was not meant for canning of foods. So, it will not work for you.

Breakfast Recipes

Corned Beef Hash

Preparation time: 15 minutes

Cooking time: 40 minutes

Total time: 55 minutes

Serves: 6 to 8 people

Recipe Ingredients:

- 1 lb. of cooked corned beef, diced
- 2 tbsp. of vegetable oil
- 1 large white onion, peeled, finely chopped
- 2 bell peppers, finely chopped
- 3 medium baking potatoes, peeled, diced
- ½ tsp. of ground black pepper
- 4 tsp. of kosher salt, divided
- 6 to 8 large eggs
- Hot sauce, for serving

Cooking Instructions:

1. Select the Sear/Sauté function on your Ninja and set to High. Then select the Start/Stop function to begin.

2. Allow the Ninja to preheat for about 5 minutes. Then add in corned beef to pot and sauté until fat has rendered for about 5 minutes.

3. Add in oil, onion, peppers, and potatoes to pot. Season with pepper and 2 tsp. of salt.

4. Sauté for about 5 to 10 minutes, until onions are translucent and peppers have softened.

5. Allow the onions and peppers to cook for another 5 minutes, without stirring, so that a crust forms on the bottom.

6. When the time is up, stir the mixture. Then, cook for another 5 minutes, without stirring.

7. After the 5 minutes, crack eggs onto the surface on the hash and season with the remaining salt.

8. Secure the crisping Lid in place and select Broil. Set time to about 10 minutes. Check eggs frequently, cooking until desired doneness.

9. When the time is up. Serve eggs and hash with hot sauce and enjoy!

Cranberry Oat Bars

Preparation time: 15 minutes

Cooking time: 30 minutes

Total time: 45 minutes

Serves: 6 to 8 people

Recipe Ingredients:

- 1 cup all-purpose flour
- 1 cup of quick-cooking rolled oats
- 1/3 cup of brown sugar
- ¼ tsp. of baking soda
- 1 stick (½ cup) butter, room temperature
- 1 cup of whole cranberry sauce

Cooking Instructions:

1. Combine the flour, oats, brown sugar, and baking soda together in a medium mixing bowl.

2. Use your hands to blend butter into mixture until it resembles coarse crumbs. Secure the crisping Lid in place.

3. Then preheat the unit by selecting Bake/Roast function. Set the temperature to 325°F, and set the time to about 5 minutes.

4. Select the Start/Stop function to begin. Reserve 1 cup of crumb mixture and set aside.

5. Grease the Ninja multi-purpose pan, press remaining mixture into the bottom of the pan.

6. Spread cranberry sauce over crumb mixture and sprinkle the 1 cup reserved mixture on top.

7. Place pan on reversible rack, ensuring that the rack is in the lower position. Once unit is preheated.

8. Place the rack with pan in your pot and secure the crisping Lid. Then select the Bake/Roast function.

9. Set the temperature to 325°F, and set time to about 30 minutes. Select Start/Stop to begin.

10. When the time is up, remove rack with pan from pot. Allow it to cool completely before cutting into bars. Serve and enjoy!

Baked Western Omelette

Preparation time: 10 minutes

Cooking time: 35 minutes

Overall time: 45 minutes

Serves: 6 to 8 people

Recipe Ingredients:

- 8 large eggs
- ½ cup of milk
- Kosher salt and pepper, to taste
- 1 cup of shredded cheddar cheese
- 1 cup of cooked ham, diced
- 1/3 cup of red bell pepper, diced
- 1/3 cup of green bell pepper, diced
- ½ cup of fresh chives, diced

Cooking Instructions:

1. Secure the crisping lid in place and preheat the unit by selecting Bake/Roast function.

2. Set the temperature to 315°F, and set the time to about 5 minutes. Then select the Start/Stop function to begin.

3. Whisk together eggs, milk, salt, and pepper together in a medium mixing bowl. Then add remaining ingredients.

4. Give everything a good stir to combine. Generously grease the bottom of the Ninja multi-purpose pan with cooking spray.

5. Pour the egg mixture into pan and place pan on reversible rack, ensure that the rack is in the lower position.

6. Once unit is preheated, place rack with pan in pot. Secure the crisping lid in place.

7. Select the Bake/Roast function and set the temperature to 315°F, set time to about 35 minutes.

8. Select the Start/Stop function to begin. After the 35 minutes. Serve omelette and enjoy!

Arroz Con Leche

Preparation time: 5 minutes

Cooking time: 7 minutes

Total time: 12 minutes

Serves: 8 to 10 people

Recipe Ingredients:

- 2 cups of long grain white rice
- 6½ cups of whole milk, cold, divided
- ½ cup of granulated sugar
- 3 strips of lime zest
- 3 cinnamon sticks
- ¼ tsp. of kosher salt
- ¾ can (10.5 oz.) sweetened condensed milk
- Ground cinnamon, for garnish

Cooking Instructions:

1. Start by placing rice, 6 cups milk, sugar, lime zest, cinnamon sticks, and salt into the pot.

2. Give everything a good stir to combine. Secure the pressure Lid in place and make sure the vent is sealed.

3. Select the Pressure function and set to cook at High Pressure for about 2 minutes.

4. Select the Start/Stop function to begin. When the time is up, allow the cooker to release pressure naturally for about 10 minutes.

5. After the natural pressure release, do a quick pressure release to release the remaining pressure.

6. Remove the Lid carefully. Add sweetened condensed milk to the pot and stir to incorporate.

7. Select the Sear/Sauté function and set to Medium. Select the Start/Stop function to begin.

8. Allow to simmer for about 5 minutes, stirring frequently. Then, remove pot carefully to a heat-safe surface.

9. Stir in the remaining milk and allow to cool for about 15 minutes. Serve warm or cool to room temperature. Serve and enjoy!

Maple-Brown Sugar Oatmeal with Apples and Raisins

Preparation time: 5 minutes

Cooking time: 14 minutes

Total time: 19 minutes

Serves: 6 to 8 people

Recipe Ingredients:

- 2 cups of plain steel cut oats
- 6 cups of water
- 3 apples, cored, cut in quarters, sliced in ½-inch pieces
- ½ cup of raisins
- 1 tsp. of ground cinnamon
- 1/3 cup of brown sugar
- 2 tbsp. of maple syrup
- 1 tbsp. of butter

Cooking Instructions:

1. Start by Placing oats, water, apples, raisins, and cinnamon into your Ninja pot.

2. Secure the pressure Lid in place and ensure that the vent is sealed. Select the Pressure function, and set to High Pressure.

3. Set time to about 10 minutes. Then select the Start/Stop function to begin. When the time is up.

4. Allow the cooker to release pressure naturally for about 10 minutes before doing a quick pressure release.

5. Remove the Lid carefully. Select the Sear/Sauté function and set to Medium High.

6. Select the Start/Stop function to begin. Add sugar, maple syrup, and butter to pot. Stir for 3 to 4 minutes, or until desired consistency is reached.

7. Serve immediately and enjoy!

Bacon & Pepper Breakfast Hash

Preparation time: 15 minutes

Cooking time: 45 minutes

Total time: 1 hour

Serves: 3 to 4 people

Recipe Ingredients:

- ½ package (8 oz.) of uncooked bacon, cut in ¼-inch pieces
- 1 small yellow onion, peeled, diced
- 1 red bell pepper, diced
- 2 russet potatoes, peeled, diced
- 1 tsp. of paprika
- 1 tsp. of black pepper, plus more for seasoning
- 1 tsp. of celery or garlic salt
- 1 tsp. of kosher salt, plus more for seasoning
- 4 large eggs

Cooking Instructions:

1. Start by removing the crisper plate from the basket and insert basket in unit.

2. Select the Roast function and preheat the unit. Set the temperature to 300°F, and set the time to about 3 minutes.

3. Select the Start/Stop function to begin. When the time is up, add bacon to the basket.

4. Select the Roast function and set temperature to 300°F, set time to about 45 minutes.

5. Then select Start/Stop function to begin. Set your Ninja to cook for about 5 minutes, or until bacon is crispy.

6. Stir occasionally during the cooking process. Add the onion, pepper, potatoes, and spices to the basket.

7. Stir to incorporate, then insert basket in unit. Set your Ninja to cook for about 35 minutes, stirring occasionally.

8. Cook until potatoes are cooked through and golden brown. Once vegetables are cooked.

9. Select the Start/Stop function to pause cooking. Then remove the basket from unit and crack four eggs onto the surface of the hash.

10. Season with additional salt and pepper, to taste. Reinsert basket and select the Start/Stop function to resume cooking.

11. Set your Ninja to cook for about 3 to 5 minutes, or until eggs are cooked to desired doneness.

12. When the time is up, serve immediately and enjoy!

Baked Nest Eggs

Preparation time: 10 minutes

Cooking time: 25 minutes

Overall time: 35 minutes

2 to 4 people **Recipe**

Ingredients:

For each nest:

- 1 slice or 2 black forest ham
- 1 large egg
- 1 tablespoon of cream
- Sprinkle with your choice of grated cheese
- Sprinkle with dried basil

Cooking Instructions:

1. Start by turning your Ninja to the Oven setting of 350°F.

2. We used a silicone muffin tin which fits on the Ninja rack. Line with ham and break egg over the top.

3. Then add the cream, sprinkle with cheese and basil. Set your Ninja to bake for about 15 to 20 minutes.

4. When the time is up, serve immediately and enjoy!

Brown Sugar & Cinnamon Oatmeal

Preparation time: 5 minutes

Cooking time: 10 minutes

Overall time: 15 minutes

Serves: 2 to 4 people

Recipe Ingredients:

- 4 cups of water
- 4 cups of quick cook oats
- 1 tablespoon of cinnamon
- ¼ cup of brown sugar
- ½ stick butter

Cooking Instructions:

1. Start by turning your Ninja to Stove Top High to boil water. Then add oats and give everything a good stir.

2. Turn off your Ninja. Add in cinnamon and brown sugar, stir everything together. Add the butter on top and let it melt.

3. Give everything a stir. Scoop into a bowl and add milk. (We use fat free).

4. Serve immediately and enjoy!

French Toast Casserole

Preparation time: 10 minutes

Cooking time: 45 minutes

Total time: 55 minutes

Serves: 4 to 6 people

Recipe Ingredients:

- 8 large eggs
- 2 cups of milk
- 1 teaspoon of cinnamon,
- ½ teaspoon of nutmeg
- 1 loaf of French bread, cubed
- 1 cup of brown sugar
- 1 stick of butter-melted together, topping

Cooking Instructions:

1. In a medium mixing bowl, beat eggs, milk, cinnamon, and nutmeg together.

2. Place the cubed French bread into a bowl and pour mixture over. Place the lid turning the bowl so it all gets absorbed.

3. Place in the refrigerator for about 6 hours. Pour into the Ninja, and put the brown sugar mixture on top.

4. Then turn the Ninja to the Oven setting of 300°F for about 45 minutes. Turn to Slow Cook Low to keep hot.

5. Serve immediately and enjoy!

Shakshuka

Preparation time: 5 minutes

Cooking time: 15 minutes

Overall time: 20 minutes

Recipe Ingredients:

- 1 tablespoon of olive oil
- 1- (14 oz.) can chickpeas
- ½ red onion, diced
- 3 cloves of garlic, minced
- 1 teaspoon of cumin
- ½ teaspoon of salt
- ¼ teaspoon of red pepper flakes
- 1- (28 oz.) can crushed tomatoes
- 4 large eggs
- 1 oz. feta
- Parsley

Cooking Instructions:

1. Turn the Ninja to Stove Top High and preheat for about 5 to 7 minutes.

2. Add the chickpeas, onion and garlic. Set your Ninja to cook for about 5 minutes. When the time is up.

3. Add the cumin, pepper flakes and salt. Give everything a good stir and add tomatoes.

4. Then crack the eggs on top. Turn to the Oven setting of 350°F and bake for about 7 minutes, or until eggs are set.

5. Garnish with feta and parsley. Serve immediately and enjoy!

Steel-Cut Oatmeal

Preparation time: 5 minutes

Cooking time: 30 minutes

Total time: 35 minutes

Serves: 2 to 4 people

Recipes Ingredients:

- 4 cups of water
- 1 cup of steel-cut oatmeal
- ¼ tsp. of salt
- ¼ tsp. of ground cinnamon
- ¼ cup of golden raisins
- ¼ cup of chopped pecans

Cooking Instructions:

1. Start by adding water to the Ninja pot and set to Stove Top High. Secure the Lid in place and bring to a boil.

2. Add in steel-cut oatmeal, salt, and ground cinnamon, give everything a good stir.

3. Set pot to Stove Top Low, remove the Lid carefully. Set Ninja to cook for about 25 to 30 minutes.

4. Stir in golden raisins and chopped pecans.

5. Serve immediately and enjoy!

Grits Southern Style

Preparation time: 10 minutes

Cooking time: 30 minutes

Overall time: 40 minutes

Serves: 2 to 4 people

Recipe Ingredients:

- ½ medium yellow onion, finely diced
- 3 slices thick-cut bacon, finely diced
- 3 tbsp. of pure maple syrup
- 4 cups of water
- 1 cup of white corn grits
- ¼ tsp. of salt
- 1 cup low-fat cheddar cheese, shredded

Cooking Instructions:

1. Set your Ninja pot to Stove Top High. Then add onion and bacon, sauté for about 8 to 10 minutes.

2. Stir occasionally during sautéing process. When the time is up, add maple syrup and cook for about 5 minutes.

3. Stir occasionally. After the 5 minutes, remove bacon and onion and keep warm.

4. Add in water and secure the Lid in place, bring to a boil. Add grits slowly, stirring the whole time.

5. Stir in salt and set your Ninja pot to Stove Top Low, cover and cook for about 15 to 20 minutes. Stir occasionally, add cheddar cheese and blend ingredients.

6. Serve immediately and enjoy.

Poultry Recipes

Chicken with Pineapple

Preparation time: 5 minutes

Cooking time: 20 minutes

Total time: 25 minutes

Serves: 2 to 4 people

Recipe Ingredients:

- 2 chicken breasts
- 4 to 6 tablespoons of General Tsao's sauce
- ½ cup of small pineapple chunks

Cooking Instructions:

1. Put the chicken in the baking pan and add some sauce on each chicken breast.

2. Add a pineapple piece. Then add the rest of the sauce on top of the pineapple. Place the pan on the rack.

3. Set the Oven to 350°F for about 20 minutes. When the time is up, served it with fresh corn on the cob and spinach.

4. Serve immediately and enjoy!

Roast Chicken

Preparation time: 5 minutes

Cooking time: 46 minutes

Total time: 51 minutes

Recipe Ingredients:

- 4 to 5 lbs. of whole chicken
- 5 cloves of garlic, peeled and crushed
- ¾ cup of hot water
- Ingredients for dry rub recipe or your own seasonings
- 2 tbsp. of butter, melted
- Parsley for garnish, optional

Cooking Instructions:

1. Clean and pat dry the chicken. Set aside. Then add in garlic and water in your Ninja Foodi pot.

2. Sprinkle the chicken generously with dry rub or own seasonings. Ensure to season the inside of chicken.

3. Set Cook & Crisp Basket in the pot, place chicken in basket breast side up. Secure the Lid and ensure vent is closed.

4. Select the Pressure function and set to cook at High Pressure for about 21 minutes.

5. When the time is up, allow the cooker to release pressure naturally for about 15 minutes.

6. After the pressure release, remove the Lid carefully. Brush chicken with melted butter and lightly sprinkle with a bit more seasoning.

7. Secure the Lid, Air Crisp at 400°F for about 20 minutes. After the 20 minutes, Let chicken rest for about 5 to 10 minutes.

8. Ensure its internal temperature reaches 165°F. Serve immediately and enjoy!

Whole Chicken

Preparation time: 15 minutes

Cooking time: 1 hour

Total time: 1 hour

Serves: 4 to 5 people

Recipe Ingredients:

- 4 pounds of whole chicken, (ours was 4.5 pounds.)
- 2 tablespoons of garlic salt
- ½ teaspoon of basil
- ½ teaspoon of onion powder
- 3 tablespoons of olive oil
- ½ teaspoon of oregano

Cooking Instructions:

1. Start by washing the chicken, Pat dry and rub olive oil on skin. Spray non-stick oil inside the air fryer basket.

2. Place the chicken into the basket with the breast side facing down. Season with half the amount of spices listed above on the side facing up.

3. Secure the Lid, select the Air Crisp function and set to cook at 360°F for about 30 minutes.

4. After the 30 minutes, flip to breast side up and spray with olive oil. Add other half of listed seasonings listed on to the breast side.

5. Set to cook for another 30 minutes at 360°F. when the time is up, allow the cooker to release pressure naturally for about 5 minutes.

6. Serve immediately and enjoy!

Turkey Paprikash

Preparation time: 10 minutes

Cooking time: 35 minutes

Total time: 45 minutes

Recipe Ingredients:

- 2 bone-in turkey legs (about 2 lbs.)
- 2 bone-in turkey thighs (about 3 lbs.)
- 4 cloves of garlic, peeled
- 2 tbsp. of sweet smoked Hungarian paprika
- ¼ cup of brine liquid from pickled jalapeños
- 1 tbsp. of kosher salt
- 1 cup of beer
- 1 cup of sour cream
- 2 tbsp. of instant flour

Cooking Instructions:

1. Add in all the recipe ingredients, except sour cream and flour, into the pot. Secure the Lid and make sure vent is closed.

2. Select the Pressure function, set to cook at High Pressure for about 20 minutes. Select the Start/Stop function to begin.

3. When the time is up, do a quick pressure release. After the pressure release remove the Lid carefully.

4. Rotate the turkey parts so they are skin-side up. Secure the Lid and select Broil function, set time to 15 minutes.

5. Select the Start/Stop function to begin. Cook until skin is blistered, brown, and crisp. When the time is up, remove turkey from the sauce and set aside to rest.

6. You can either shred the turkey once cool and reheat in the sauce or drizzle the sauce over the turkey.

7. Select the Sear/Sauté function, set cooker to cook to High. Select the Start/Stop function to begin.

8. Add in sour cream and flour to the liquid in the pot, whisking constantly. Bring mixture to a boil, once boiling.

9. Select the Start/Stop function to cancel Sear/Sauté. Ladle the sauce over the turkey. Serve immediately and enjoy!

Garlic and Parm crusted chicken with roasted potatoes

Preparation time: 5 minutes

Cooking time: 30 minutes

Total time: 35 minutes

Serves: 1

Recipe Ingredients:

- 5 lbs. of cubed potatoes
- 1 lb. of chicken breast
- 1.5 sticks butter
- 1 cup of panko bread crumbs
- 1 medium egg
- 1 tablespoon of Italian seasonings
- ½ cup of shredded Parm cheese
- 1 tablespoon of garlic powder
- ½ tablespoon of salt
- ½ tablespoon of pepper

Cooking Instructions:

1. Stir in garlic powder and Italian seasonings in your pot. Then place chopped potatoes in the bottom of the Ninja Foodi.

2. Pour butter over the potatoes, ensure that they are all coated thoroughly. Mix panko and parm cheese together.

3. Whisk the egg and dip chicken breast in egg then in panko Mix. Place a trivet on top of the potatoes. Place your chicken breast on top of the trivet.

4. Select the Pressure function, set to cook at High Pressure for about 10 minutes. When the time is up.

5. Do a quick pressure release and remove the Lid carefully. cook on air fry at 390°F for about 15 minutes.

6. After the 15 minutes, serve immediately and enjoy!

Baked Cajun Chicken Thighs and Drumsticks

Preparation time: 35 minutes

Cooking time: 15 minutes

Total time: 50 minutes

Cooking Ingredients:

- 3 pounds of chicken thighs and drumsticks
- Juice of 2 lemons
- 125ml of hot chicken stock
- Salt & pepper

Cajun Seasoning:

- 1½ tablespoon of oil
- 1 tablespoon of salt
- 1 tablespoon of garlic powder
- 1 tablespoon of smoked paprika
- 1 teaspoon of cayenne pepper
- 1 teaspoon of onion powder
- ¼ teaspoon of white pepper
- ¼ teaspoon of black pepper
- ½ teaspoon of dried oregano
- ¼ teaspoon of dried thyme

Cooking Instructions:

1. Start by combining the lemon, stock, water, salt and pepper in the cooking pot.

2. Season the chicken. Add the Cajun seasoning ingredients along with the chicken to a large bowl and marinade for an hour.

3. Place into the air crisp basket and then into the cooking pot. Spray with cooking oil.

4. Secure the Lid in place. Set to Air fry at 200ºC for about 15 minutes. Remove once done.

5. Serve immediately and enjoy!

Chicken & Wild Rice with Carrots

Preparation time: 5 minutes

Cooking time: 55 minutes

Total time: 1 hour

Serves: 5 to 6 people

Recipe Ingredients:

- 2 cups of chicken broth or stock
- 1 pound of carrots
- 1½ cups of wild rice blend
- ¼ cup of butter, salted and cut into 9 pats
- 2 pounds of chicken thighs frozen boneless/skinless

Seasoning Blend:

- 1½ teaspoon of sea salt
- 1 teaspoon of black pepper
- ½ teaspoon of poultry seasoning
- 1 teaspoon of thyme leaves dried
- ¾ teaspoon of garlic powder
- ¾ teaspoon of onion powder

Cooking Instructions:

1. Start by adding the chicken stock to the inner pot. Peel and cut the carrots into large pieces and place into the fry basket.

2. Set your Ninja Foodi to cook at High Pressure for about 2 minutes. Mix up the seasoning blend. Cut butter into 9 pats.

3. After the 2 minutes, do a quick pressure release and remove the basket with the carrots. Set aside.

4. Rinse the wild rice blend under cold water for 1 to 2 minutes. Add rice to chicken stock in the bottom of the inner pot.

5. Sprinkle with 1/3 of the seasoning blend. Place 3 pats of butter on top. Layer the frozen chicken thighs on top of the rice.

6. We break the pats into smaller pieces to place one on each piece of chicken. Secure the Lid in place.

7. Set your Ninja Foodi to cook at High Pressure for about 30 minutes. After the 30 minutes.

8. Do a quick pressure release. Add the carrots directly on top of the chicken. Sprinkle with remaining seasoning and butter pats.

9. Set your Ninja Foodi to the bake function, set to bake at 375°F for about 8 to 15 minutes.

10. When the time is up, serve immediately and enjoy!

Breads and Baker Goods

Salted Caramel Chip Cookies

Preparation time: 20 minutes

Cooking time: 10 minutes

Overall time: 30 minutes

Serves: 8 to 10 people

Recipe Ingredients

- ¼ cup of unsalted butter, softened
- ½ tsp. of vanilla extract
- ¼ cup of light brown sugar, firmly packed
- 2 tbsp. of granulated sugar
- ½ tsp. of salt
- 1 cup of all-purpose flour
- ¼ tsp. of baking soda
- 1 extra-large egg, lightly beaten
- 2/3 cup of caramel or toffee bits

Cooking Instructions:

1. Start by preheating your oven to 350°F. Line a baking sheet with parchment paper, set aside.

2. Position the Dough Blade Assembly in the 64-oz. Precision Processor. Add in all the recipe ingredients, except caramel or toffee bits.

3. Select Dough function. Add caramel or toffee bits to the 64-oz. Precision Processor and select Chop function.

4. Carefully scrape down sides of bowl with spatula. Scoop dough by the tablespoonful onto prepared baking sheet 2 inches apart.

5. Set your Ninja to Bake for about 8 to 10 minutes, or until light golden brown. When the time is up, serve immediately and enjoy!

Banana Bread

Preparation time: 15 minutes

Cooking time: 40 minutes

Total time: 55 minutes

Serves: 1 to 3 people

Recipe Ingredients:

- 2 cups of all-purpose flour
- 1 tsp. of baking soda
- ¼ tsp. of kosher salt
- 1 stick (½ cup) butter, softened
- ¾ cup of dark brown sugar
- 2 large eggs, beaten
- 3 medium ripe bananas, mashed

Cooking Instructions:

1. Secure the crisping Lid in place and preheat the unit by selecting Bake/Roast function.

2. Set the temperature to 325°F, and set the time to cook for about 5 minutes. Select the Start/Stop function to begin.

3. In a medium mixing bowl, stir together flour, baking soda, and salt. Then in a separate mixing bowl, beat together butter and brown sugar.

4. Add in eggs and bananas, give everything a good stir to combine. Slowly add dry mixture to wet mixture.

5. Stir them together until well combined. Grease the Ninja loaf pan and add butter to pan. Once unit has preheated.

6. Place pan on reversible rack, ensure that the rack is in the lower position. Secure the crisping Lid in place.

7. Select the Bake/Roast function and set temperature to 325°F, set time to about 40 minutes.

8. Select the Start/Stop function to begin. When the time is up, remove pan from pot and place on a cooling rack.

9. Allow bread to cool for about 30 minutes. Serve immediately and enjoy!

Oatmeal Raisin Bread

Preparation time: 10 minutes

Cooking time: 40 minutes

Overall time: 50 minutes

Serves: 8 to 10 persons

Recipe Ingredients:

- ¾ cup of warm water (110 to 115 °F)
- 1 tbsp. of sugar
- 1 package (¼ oz.) active dry yeast
- 2 tbsp. of vegetable oil
- 1 tsp. of kosher salt
- 1 cup of unbleached bread flour
- ½ cup of whole wheat flour
- ½ cup of quick-cooking oats
- 1 cup of dark raisins

Cooking Instructions:

1. Place the water, sugar, and yeast in a small mixing bowl. Allow to sit for about 5 minutes.

2. Using the single dough blade, place the yeast mixture, oil, salt, flours, oats, and raisins.

3. Blend them for about 20 seconds, until well combined. Remove the dough ball and place in a mixing bowl that has been coated with vegetable oil.

4. Cover with plastic wrap and let sit in a warm place for about 2 hours. Lightly coat a loaf pan with cooking spray.

5. Form dough into a loaf and place in pan. Let rise for about 2 hours or until double in size.

6. Then preheat your oven to 350 °F. Set Ninja to Bake for about 35 to 40 minutes or until golden brown. When the time is up, allow to cool before serving.

7. Serve immediately and enjoy!

Apple Cherry Pastries with Pistachios

Preparation time: 30 minutes

Cooking time: 1 hours 30 minutes

Overall time: 2 hours

Serves: 6 to 8 people

Recipe Ingredients:

- 1 lemon
- 8 apples (about 3 lbs.), peeled and cut into ¼-inch slices
- ½ cup of dried cherries
- 1 cup of sugar
- 1 package (3.4 oz.) vanilla instant pudding and pie filling mix
- 3 cups of cold milk
- 2 packages (10 oz. each) frozen puff pastry shells, prepared according to package directions, cooled
- ½ cup of shelled pistachio nuts, chopped

Cooking Instructions:

1. Grate ½ tsp. of zest from lemon. Stir apples, cherries, sugar, and lemon zest in pot.

2. Set your Ninja to Slow Cook High for about 2 to 3 hours. Secure the Lid in place and cook until apples are tender.

3. In a medium mixing bowl, beat pudding mix and milk for about 2 minutes or until mixture is thickened.

4. Divide apple mixture among pastry shells. Top with pudding mixture and sprinkle with nuts.

5. Serve immediately and enjoy!

Apples and Prosciutto in Sweet Potato Pastry

Preparation time: 10 minutes

Cooking time: 45 minutes

Overall time: 55 minutes

Serves: 5 to 6 people

Recipe Ingredients:

- 1 sweet potato pastry
- 6 large eggs
- 1 large Fuji apple, peeled, cored and roughly chopped
- 3-ounce prosciutto, cooked and chopped
- Pinch nutmeg
- Salt and pepper to taste

Cooking Instructions:

1. Start by preheating your oven to 400°F. Coat a 10-inch quiche or pie pan with cooking spray.

2. Press the potato pastry evenly onto the sides and bottom. Set your Ninja to Bake for about 8 to 10 minutes.

3. When the time is up, remove and reduce the heat to 350°F. Place the eggs and apple in the 40 oz. Processing Bowl.

4. Pulse until the apple is evenly chopped. Add the prosciutto, salt, pepper and nutmeg.

5. Pulse for about 2 to 3 times. Pour into the pastry and bake for about 35 to 45 minutes, until the centre is set.

6. Cut into wedges and serve while warm. Serve and enjoy!

Peter Cotton Tail Carrot Muffins

Preparation time: 5 minutes

Cooking time: 15 minutes

Gross time: 20 minutes

Serves: 3 to 4 people

Recipe Ingredients:

- ¾ cup of all-purpose flour
- ½ cup of whole wheat flour
- 2 tablespoon of wheat germ
- 1 teaspoon of ground cinnamon
- 1 teaspoon of baking powder
- ½ teaspoon of baking soda
- Pinch salt
- 1/3 cup of vegetable oil
- ½ cup of buttermilk
- 2 large eggs
- ¾ cup of light brown sugar
- 2 cups of grated carrots

Cooking Instructions:

1. Preheat your oven to 350°F. Place all the ingredients, except carrots, into the 48 oz. Blender, blend until well combined.

2. Add in carrots to the blender and pulse 2 to 3 times until well-combined. Line a muffin pan with paper cups and spoon the carrot batter into the cups.

3. Bake for about 18 to 20 minutes, when the time is up. Serve immediately and enjoy!

Veggie Quiche Cheddar Muffins

Preparation time: 5 minutes

Cooking time: 25 minutes

Total time: 30 minutes Serves:

2 to 4 people

Recipe Ingredients:

- 1½ cups of spinach, rinsed and dried
- 4 large eggs
- 4 egg whites
- ½ small red bell pepper, seeded and roughly chopped
- ¼ medium red onion, peeled and roughly chopped
- ¼ cup of diced mushrooms
- ¼ cup of cheddar cheese, shredded

Cooking Instructions

1. Set Ninja to oven, heat to 350°F. Place ingredients into the 40 oz. Blender and blend until well-chopped and combined. Line a muffin pan with baking cups

2. spray with non-stick cooking spray. Spoon the egg mixture into the individual muffin cups and bake for 20-25 minutes.

3. Serve immediately and Enjoy!

Chunky Monkey Cookies

Preparation time: 30 minutes

Cooking time: 10 minutes

Overall time: 40 minutes

Serves: 8 to 10 people

Recipe Ingredients:

- 3 ripe bananas, peeled
- 2 cups regular or quick-cooking oatmeal
- ¼ cup chunky peanut butter
- ¼ cup cocoa powder
- 1/3 cup unsweetened applesauce
- 1 tsp. vanilla extract

Cooking Instructions:

1. Having set your Ninja to oven mode, Preheat oven to 350°F.

2. Place the paddle attachment into the 72-ounce blender, add the bananas first.

3. Once bananas are mashed, add the remaining ingredients and stir until they are well combined.

4. Allow cookies to sit for 20 minutes then drop tablespoon sized cookies onto a cookie sheet. Bake for 10 minutes.

5. Chunky Monkey Cookies is ready, serve and enjoy!

Cranberry Orange Cake

Preparation time: 30 minutes

Cooking time: 60 minutes

Overall time: 1hr; 30 minutes.

Serves: 4 to 8 people

Recipe Ingredients:

- 2 ½ cups all-purpose white flour
- 2 tsp. of baking powder
- ½ tsp. of baking soda
- ½ tsp. of salt
- 1 cup of brown sugar
- ¼ cup of granulated sugar
- ½ cup of butter, melted and cooled to room temperature
- ½ cup of low-fat sour cream
- ¼ cup of orange juice
- 3 eggs
- 1 tsp. of vanilla extract
- 1 cup of dried cranberries, chopped and soaked in ½ cup orange liqueur
- ½ of cup pecans, toasted
- Cooking spray

Cooking Instructions:

1. In a large bowl, combine flour, baking powder, baking soda and salt, and set aside.

2. Making use of the Bottom Blades in the Pitcher, add the remaining ingredients, except the cranberries and pecans.

3. Select Speed 1 and flip the switch to start. Then slowly increase to Speed 5 and blend until it is well-combined together.

4. Pour the sour cream/egg mixture into the flour mixture in the bowl, stirring well to incorporate. Drain cranberries and add into the butter. Add the toasted pecans and stir continuously until well mixed.

5. Lightly coat a 9 x 5-inch loaf pan with cooking spray. Pour butter into pan and bake at 350°F for 60 minutes until a knife inserted into centre comes out clean.

6. Now serve immediately and enjoy!

Queensland Banana Bread

Preparation time: 15 minutes

Cooking time: 40 minutes

Total time: 55 minutes

Serves: 1 to 3 people

Recipe Ingredients:

- ¼ cup of butter
- 1 egg
- ¾ cup of sugar
- 2 bananas, peeled and cut in half,
- 3 tablespoons of milk,
- ½ teaspoon of baking soda,
- ½ teaspoon of baking powder,
- 2 cups of all-purpose flour,
- ½ cup of macadamia nuts, chopped

Cooking Instructions:

1. Set your Ninja to oven mode, heat to 350°F. Then Fit the dough paddle into the Processor Bowl

2. Place the butter, egg, sugar, bananas and milk inside and mix until well combined.

3. Add the powder, soda, flour and macadamias and mix again briefly. Lightly coat a loaf pan with cooking spray and spoon the bread into the pan.

4. Bake for 40 minutes until a toothpick comes out clean in the middle. Serve immediately and enjoy!

Mediterranean Focaccia

Preparation time: 35 minutes

Cooking time: 20 minutes Overall

time: 55 minutes.

Serves: 4 to 6 people

Recipe Ingredients

- 1 Classic Pizza Dough
- ½ Cup of jarred in oil, sun-dried tomatoes, chopped, divided
- ½ Cup of pitted kalamata olives, divided
- ½ Cup of kasseri cheese, shredded, divided
- 2 Teaspoons of fresh oregano leaves,
- ½ Teaspoon of red chile flakes,
- ¼ cup olive oil

Cooking Instructions:

1. Merge 2 tbsp. each sun-dried tomato, olives, & kasseri cheese and set aside. Lightly oil a baking sheet and sprinkle with corn meal.

2. Turn dough out onto a lightly floured work surface and knead in remaining sundried tomatoes, olives, and cheese, and add the oregano and chile flakes.

3. Use palms to stretch and press dough into an oblong, about ½ - inch thick. Transfer to prepared baking sheet, cover and let rise for 30 minutes.

4. Set your Ninja to oven mode, to preheat at 400°F. Dimple dough with fingertips.

5. Drizzle dough with olive oil and top with tomato, olive and cheese mixture. Bake for about 20 minutes, until colour turns golden brown.

6. Serve immediately and enjoy while hot.

Beef, Pork & Lamb Recipes

Bacon Cheeseburger Meatloaf

Preparation time: 10 minutes

Cooking time: 30 minutes

Total time: 40 minutes Serves:

5 to 7 people

Recipe Ingredients:

- 2 pounds of hamburger
- 2 cloves of garlic, finely minced (We used a micro-plane)
- 2 tablespoons of onion, finely chopped
- 3 tablespoons of Worcestershire sauce
- 3 to 5 pieces of cooked crumbled bacon
- 1 cup of shredded cheese
- Salt and pepper to taste

Cooking Instructions:

1. In a medium mixing bowl, mix all the recipe Ingredients together, and form into a loaf.

2. Set your Ninja to Oven mode, set the temperature to 350°F, and place the loaf on rack.

3. Adjust the timer to bake for about 30 minutes, when the time is up. Serve immediately and enjoy.

Barbeque Sauce

Preparation time: 10 minutes

Cooking time: 20 minutes

Gross time:30minutes

Serve: 2 to 4 people

Recipe Ingredients:

- 1¼ cups of apple cider vinegar
- 2 tbsp. of Worcestershire sauce
- 2 tbsp. of peanut butter
- 1 tsp. of salt (I used sea salt)
- ¼ cup of lemon juice
- 1 tsp. of pepper
- 2 tbsp. of Chili powder – (we used green Chile Powder instead of red and omitted the salt)
- 4 tbsp. of butter

Cooking Instructions:

1. Set your Ninja to boiling mode, add all ingredients to boil and stir continuously.

2. Lower the heat and simmer for about 15 minutes.

3. Serve immediately and enjoy!

Beef & Broccoli (Slow Cook)

Preparation time: 30 minutes

Cooking time: 8 hours

Overall time: 8 hours 30 minutes

Serves: 2 to 4 people

Recipe Ingredients:

- 1 pound of boneless beef chuck roast, sliced into thin strips
- 1 cup of beef consommé
- ½ cup of soy sauce
- 1/3 of cup brown sugar
- 1 tbsp. of sesame oil
- 3 garlic cloves, minced
- 2 tbsp. of corn starch
- 2 tbsp. of sauce from the crock pot after being cooked
- Fresh broccoli florets (as many as desired)
- Hot cooked rice

Cooking Instruction:

1. Place beef in your Ninja.

2. In a small bowl, mix up consommé, soy sauce, brown sugar, oil, and garlic. Pour over beef. Set Ninja to slow cook function and cook for 8 hours.

3. In a cup, stir corn starch and sauce from the Ninja pot until smooth. Add to the pot. Stir well to mix up together. Add broccoli to the Ninja pot. Stir to combine.

4. Cover and cook an additional 30 minutes on high (the sauce has to boil for it to thicken).

5. Serve over hot cooked rice and enjoy!

Beef & Noodles

Preparation time: 20 minutes

Cooking time: 40 minutes

Total time: 60 minutes Serves:

2 to 4 people

Recipe Ingredients:

- 1 pounds extra lean ground beef
- 1 can of (10.75 oz.) Cream of Mushroom condensed soup
- 1½ cans of water
- 1 small chopped onion (optional)
- Dash of: ground pepper, garlic powder, onion powder & Tony Chachere's (optional)
- ½ (12 oz.) bag of No Yolk egg noodles

Cooking Instructions:

1. Set Ninja to Stove mode, select the pressure function and set to cook at High pressure. Add the beef, onions and seasonings and stir gently.

2. Gently put the lid on and cook until the beef is brown, stirring continuously. Add the soup and water, stir. Add the egg noodles, stir gently.

3. Then cook with the lid off until the noodles are done and the mixture has thickened.

4. Serve immediately and enjoy while hot.

Pork Cube Steak

Preparation time: 30 minutes

Cooking time: 1 hour 30 minutes

Overall time: 2 hours

Serves: 4 to 6 people

Recipe Ingredients:

- 4 cubed of pork steak
- 1 packet of onion soup
- ½ stick of butter
- ½ cup of water

Cooking Directions:

1. Start by seasoning and breading the pork, put oil in the Ninja (enough to brown).

2. Once browned, add the soup, butter and water. Then set Ninja to Slow Cook mode, select pressure function and cook at high pressure for 2 hours.

3. Also, go easy on the salt when seasoning it, the powered onion soup mix has a good amount.

4. Ready to serve and enjoy.

Pork Loin with Peaches & Rosemary

Preparation time: 15 minutes

Cooking time: 1 hour 15 minutes

Total time:1 hour 30 minutes

Serves: 4 to 8 people

Recipe Ingredients:

- 2.5 to 3 pounds of Pork Loin
- 8 ounces of jar peach preserves
- 2 medium yellow onions
- 1 small bag of new potatoes
- 3 pounds of peaches
- Fresh rosemary
- Salt and pepper – to taste
- Olive oil

Cooking Directions:

1. Set your Ninja to Stove Top High-pressure function. Add the olive oil to heat up.

2. Sear the pork loin on all sides. Dice one onion and 2 peaches and place into a medium sized bowl.

3. Add ½ jar peach preserves and stir continuously until it's well mixed. Cut the other onion into fourths and halve the remaining peaches.

4. Then add the potatoes, onions and peaches to the Ninja pot. Spread the mixture from the bowl onto the pork loin and over the potatoes, peaches and onions.

5. Turn your Ninja to 350°F. Cook the pork loin for 25 minutes per pound. (In this case 1 hour 15 minutes).

6. Serve immediately and enjoy.

Pork Roast

Preparation time: 10 minutes

Cooking time: 8 hours

Total time: 8 hours 10 minutes.

Serves: 4 to 8 people

Recipe Ingredients:

- 1 pork roast
- Olive oil
- Jamaican Jerk seasoning
- Vegetable broth or use any marinade you wish

Cooking Directions:

1. Turn the Ninja to Stove Top, select pressure function and set at High pressure. Season the roast. Add the olive oil and sear the roast.

2. Add the vegetable broth to the pot with the roast. Turn Ninja setting to Slow Cook, cook on Low pressure function and cook for about 8 hours.

3. Serve immediately and enjoy.

Pork Sofrito

Preparation time: 5 minutes

Cooking time: 4 hours

Total time: 4 hours 5 minutes.

Serves: 2 to 4 people

Ingredients:

- 3 large Pork country ribs
- 1 jar of Sofrito sauce
- ½ jar of chicken broth

Cooking Instructions:

1. Turn your Ninja to Stove mode, select pressure function and set to cook at High pressure and brown the ribs.

2. Pour the sauce and broth over all. After that turn your Ninja to Slow Cook Low function and cook for about 4 hours.

3. Serve immediately and enjoy.

Pork Tenderloin Stroganoff

Preparation time: 15 minutes

Cooking time: 20 minutes

Total time: 35 minutes

Serves: 4 to 6 people

Recipe Ingredients:

- Pork tenderloin, sliced in ½" thick pieces
- 3 tbsp. of butter
- 1 can of cream mushroom soup
- ½ can of water
- 1 small jar of sliced mushrooms
- 1 cup of sour
- Cooked egg noodles

Cooking Instructions:

1. Turn Ninja setting to Stove mode, Select the Pressure function and set to cook at Low Pressure and brown pork in butter.

2. Add soup, water and mushrooms and stir until it is well mixed together. Set your Ninja to slow cook and cook for 20 minutes or until meat is tender.

3. Add sour cream before removing from heat and immediately pour over cooked egg noodles.

4. serve and enjoy.

Pulled Pork

Preparation time: 12 minutes

Cooking time: 8 hours

Total time: 8 hrs. 12 minutes

Serves: 8 to 10 people

Recipe Ingredients:

- 4 to 5 pounds
- 1 large onion, sliced
- ¼ to ½ cup of apple cider vinegar
- BBQ sauce
- Rub: equal amounts – or to taste
- Garlic powder
- Onion powder
- Paprika
- Chili powder
- Chipotle powder
- Salt and pepper
- Brown sugar

Cooking Instruction:

1. Start by rubbing the seasonings into your pork. Place the onion slices in your Ninja pot and add the pork shoulder on top.

2. Pour the apple cider vinegar on top. Squeeze your desired amount of sauce over the pork.

3. Turn your Ninja to Slow Cook mode and cook at Low pressure for 8 hours. Remove and shred.

4. Now serve and enjoy.

Ranch Pork Chops

Preparation time: 5 minutes

Cooking time: 4 hours

Total time: 4 hrs. 5 minutes

Serves: 6 to 8 people

Recipe Ingredients:

1. Boneless Chops (we used thin cut but any would work)
2. 1 packet of ranch dressing
3. 1 can of cream of chicken
4. Olive Oil for browning

Cooking Instructions:

1. Turn Ninja to Stove mode and set to High pressure function to Brown chops each side for about 2 min.

2. Now after that switch Ninja to Slow Cook, and select Low cook pressure function. Sprinkle ranch packet evenly over chops.

3. In a separate medium mixing bowl prepare soup (mix soup and water continuously until it is smooth).

4. Then pour soup over chops. Set Ninja to Slow Cook mode and cook at low pressure for about 4 hours.

5. Serve immediately and enjoy!

Sage & Parmesan Crusted Pork Loin Chops

Preparation time: 15 minutes

Cooking time: 30 minutes

Overall time: 45 minutes

Serves: 2 to 4 people

Recipe Ingredients:

- ½ cup of grated parmesan cheese
- ½ cup of bread crumbs
- Pinch rubbed sage
- Pinch smoked paprika
- ½ teaspoon of Italian seasoning
- Salt and pepper
- Pork loin chops
- Olive oil

Cooking Directions:

1. Mix parmesan cheese, bread crumbs and seasonings on a plate.

2. Rub the chops with a little olive oil. Press cheese mixture into chops. Place directly onto the rack.

3. Place rack in the Ninja. Set Ninja to dry baked function. Set the Oven to 425°F for 15 minutes.

4. After 15 minutes, turn down your Ninja oven to 375°F and bake for another for 30 minutes.

5. Serve immediately and enjoy

Lamb & Onions

Preparation time: 8 minutes

Cooking time: 4 hours

Total time: 4 hrs. 8 minutes

Serves: 2 to 4 people

Recipe Ingredients:

- 2 pieces of lamb shoulder
- 1 or 2 onions, sliced
- 4 cloves of garlic, chopped
- 1 can of chicken broth
- Salt and pepper to taste
- 2 tbsp. of butter
- 1 tbsp. of olive oil
- Flour to coat

Cooking Instructions:

1. Start by seasoning lamb with salt, pepper, and lightly flour.

2. Add butter and olive oil to your Ninja. Brown lamb on Stove Top High-pressure settings. Add the onions, garlic and chicken broth.

3. Turn Ninja to Slow Cook mode, select the pressure function and set to cook at low pressure for 4 hours or until tender.

4. Serve over wide egg noodles and enjoy.

Lamb Chops with Betty Crocker Scalloped Potatoes

Preparation time: 10 minutes

Cooking time: 40 minutes

Overall time: 50 minutes

Serves: 2 to 4 people

Recipe Ingredients:

- 2 to 3 shoulder chops
- Salt and pepper
- ¼ cup of brown sugar
- 2 to 3 pineapple slices.

Cooking Instructions:

1. Set your Ninja to oven mode and preheat for 10 minutes at 375°F.

2. Place chops in cooking pot, add pineapple and some pineapple juice.

3. Cook for 40 minutes. You can use some of the juice to baste the chops.

4. Serve immediately and enjoy.

Lamb Roast

Preparation time: 20 minutes

Cooking time: 4 hours

Gross time: 4 hrs. 20 minutes

Serves: 2 to 4 people

Recipe Ingredients:

- Lamb
- Olive oil
- Onion
- Mushrooms
- ½ cup of tomato sauce
- Worcestershire sauce
- 5 tbsp. of peach chutney
- Salt & black pepper
- curry
- 2 tsp. of sugar
- Carrots
- Potatoes
- Beef stock cornflower (to thicken)

Cooking Instructions:

1. Cut and brown the lamb in olive oil, then set Ninja to Stove mode, Select the Pressure function and set to cook at High Pressure.

2. Sauté onions and mushrooms together with meat. Add the sauce: tomato sauce, Worcestershire sauce, peach chutney, salt, black pepper, curry and sugar and cook until the sauce thickens.

3. After sauce thickens, add the carrots, potatoes and beef stock to cover all ingredients.

4. Turn your Ninja to Slow Cook mode, Select the Pressure function and set to cook at High Pressure for 4 hours. Then add cornflower to thicken the sauce.

5. Serve and enjoy your meal.

Loin Lamb Chops with Baby Carrots, Potatoes & Onions

Preparation time: 15 minutes

Cooking time: 35 minutes

Overall time: 45 minutes

Serves: 2 to 5 people

Recipe Ingredients:

1. Onion, potatoes, carrots,
2. Seasonings to taste

Cooking Directions:

1. On Stove Top High pressure, sauté the onions potatoes and carrots in the pot with a little bit of butter.

2. Remove and add the lamb to the Ninja and brown. Remove the lamb to the multipurpose pan and place the vegetables.

3. Add 3 cups of liquid to the pot. Place your rack and the multipurpose pan. Then turn your Ninja to the Oven setting of 350°F for 35 minutes.

4. Gently place the lid and bring it out great.

5. Serve immediately and enjoy.

Beef Bulgogi

Preparation time: 30 minutes

Cooking time: 2 hours 30 minutes

Overall time: 3 hours

Serves: 2 to 4 persons

Recipe Ingredients:

- 3 pounds thinly slice round steak
- 2 cups of soy sauce low sodium
- 1 ¾ cup of brown sugar
- 1 teaspoon of garlic from the jar

Cooking Instructions:

1. Mix all ingredients together, set your Ninja to Slow cook mode, Select the Pressure function and set to cook at Low Pressure for about 3 hours.

2. Switch Ninja to Cook on Stove Low pressure. Add a corn starch slurry to thicken.

3. Just before serving, add about 3 or 4 green onions and sprinkle it with sesame seeds.

4. Serve with rice and lettuce to make wraps. Enjoy!!

Beef Short Ribs

Preparation time: 1 hour

Cooking time: 6 hours

Total time: 7 hours

Serves: 2 to 4 people

Recipe Ingredients:

- 2 to 3 pounds of boneless beef short ribs
- 2 bottles of A1 steakhouse marinade

Cooking Directions:

1. Turn Ninja to Stove mode, select pressure function and set to sear the ribs on Stove Top High in a little olive oil.

2. Pour in the marinade. Turn Ninja to Slow Cook mode pressure function and cook at low pressure for about 7 to 8 hours.

3. Serve immediately and enjoy!

Beef Shoulder Roast

Preparation time: 1 hour

Cooking time: 5 hours

Overall time: 6 hours

Serves: 4 to 8 people

Recipe Ingredients:

- 3 to 4 lbs. (or larger) beef shoulder roasts
- Olive oil
- Salt and pepper, to taste
- Roasted garlic seasonings
- Herb seasonings, to taste
- 1 Cream of celery soup
- 1 Cream of mushroom soup with
- 3 tbsp. of Worcestershire sauce

Cooking Directions:

1. Turn your Ninja to Stove mode and set to Top High-pressure function to heat as you are preparing your roast with the seasonings.

2. Add some oil and brown roast on all sides. Turn your Ninja to Slow Cook to cook on Low pressure, then add the soups and Worcestershire sauce.

3. Set timer to cook for about 6 to 7 hours. When the time is up.

4. Serve immediately and enjoy!

Rice & Pasta Recipes

Chicken Ravioli

Preparation time: 15 minutes

Cooking time: 25 minutes overall

time: 40 minutes

Serves: 2 to 4 people

Recipe Ingredients:

- 1 bag of refrigerated chicken ravioli
- 24 oz. jar of marinara
- ½ cup of water
- A few dollops of ricotta cheese and some mozzarella

Cooking Instructions:

1. Add all of the ingredients, except cheesed and stir continuously until the ingredients are well mixed together.

2. Turn your Ninja to the Oven setting of 250°F for 15 minutes. After the 15 minutes, add the cheeses and cook for 10 more minutes, or until tender.

3. Serve immediately and enjoy!

Chicken & Rice Bake

Preparation time: 15 minutes

Cooking time: 45 minutes

Total time: 60 minutes Serves:

2 to 8 people

Recipe Ingredients:

- 2 large chicken breasts cut in half
- 2 cups of white rice
- 1 box of chicken broth
- 1 bag of frozen broccoli and cauliflower
- Salt, pepper and paprika to taste

Cooking Directions:

1. Set your Ninja to oven mode of 350°F. Add rice, stock, chicken and veggies in the Ninja.

2. After that, add plenty of paprika and a bit of salt and pepper. Cook for about 45 minutes or until rice is tender.

3. Serve immediately and enjoy hot.

Chicken & Rice Casserole

Preparation time: 10 minutes

Cooking time: 25 minutes

Gross time: 35 minutes

Serves: 2 to 8 people

Recipe Ingredients:

- 2 tbsp. of unsalted butter
- 2 cloves of garlic, finely chopped
- 4 scallions, sliced
- 2 cups of broccoli florets
- 2 cups of shredded rotisserie chicken (skin removed)
- 1 cup of medium-grain white rice
- 1 plum of tomato, chopped
- Kosher salt and freshly ground pepper
- 2 cups of low-sodium chicken broth
- ¼ cup of sour cream
- 1 cup of diced dill havarti cheese (about 4 oz.)
- ¼ cup of grated parmesan cheese (about 1 oz.)

Cooking Instructions:

1. Select the Sear/Sauté function on your Ninja, set your Ninja on Stove Top High and Sauté the garlic and onions.

2. Add the rest of your ingredients and switch your Ninja to Oven Mode at 425°F for 20 minutes.

3. Sprinkle with the remaining havarti and parmesan, then broil about 2 minutes until it turns golden completely.

4. Then Sprinkle with the reserved scallions. Now serve and enjoy your delicious meal hot!

Chicken Fried Rice

Preparation time: 20 minutes

Cooking time: 3 hours

Total time: 3 hours 20 minutes

Recipe Ingredients:

- 3 large Chicken breasts
- Salt and pepper, to taste
- ½ Bag of frozen peas and carrots
- 2 Cups of minute rice & 2 cups water
- 2 to 3 tbsp. each of Teriyaki and soy sauce
- 3 Eggs

Cooking Directions:

1. Add the salted and peppered chicken to the Ninja pot.

2. Turn Ninja to Slow Cook Low for 3 hours, or until temperature reaches 165°F on a digital probe. Remove the peppered chicken and shred.

3. Set Ninja to Stove Top Low/Medium setting, then add the eggs to the Ninja using Scramble until done, then remove.

4. Add the rice and water, (a little more water may be needed, check and stir).

5. Add your vegetables. Now when rice is cooked, return the chicken and eggs. Stir in the sauce.

6. Serve immediately and enjoy.

Alfredo Three Cheese Bow Tie Chicken

Preparation time: 20 minutes

Cooking time: 30 minutes

Gross time: 50 minutes

Serve: 2 to 4 people

Recipe Ingredients:

- 14 ounces of jars Prego 3 Artisan Alfredo sauce
- 4 boneless, skinless chicken breast, cut in cubes
- ½ cup of green peas
- ½ cup of yellow corn
- ½ tbsp. of real bacon bits
- 4 cups of chicken broth
- 1 pounds of bow tie pasta

Cooking Instructions:

1. Set your Ninja to Stove mode and set at Top High pressure to brown your chicken cubes.

2. Add remaining ingredients to Chicken. Turn to the Oven setting of 300°F for 30 minutes, or until pasta is tender.

3. Serve immediately and enjoy!

Aunt Jill's Cheese Grits

Preparation time: 7 minutes

Cooking time: 25 minutes

Overall time: 32 minutes

Serves: 2 to 4 people

Recipe Ingredients:

- 2 cups of water
- 1¼ cups of milk
- 1 tsp. of salt
- 1 cup of quick cooking grits
- ½ cup of plus 1 tbsp. butter
- 1/3 cup of diced green onions
- 4 ounces of processed cheddar cheese, cubed (Velveeta)
- ¼ tsp. of garlic powder
- 2½ cups of shredded cheddar cheese
- 1 (10-ounces) can diced tomatoes and green chilies with liquid (Ro-Tel)

Cooking Instructions:

1. Select Sear/Sauté on your Ninja and Sauté green onions in 1 tablespoon butter for a minute or so.

2. Now add remaining ingredients, reserving ½ cup cheddar. After that, cook at 350°F for 25 minutes, stirring occasionally.

3. Sprinkle reserved cheddar on top, close lid for a few minutes until the cheese melts.

4. Wow! Cheese is ready, serve and enjoy.

Baked Pasta

Preparation time: 15 minutes

Cooking time: 45

Total time: 60 minutes Serves:

2 to 8 people

Recipe Ingredients:

- 1 lb. of ground beef or sausage browned & drained of fat
- Sliced pepperoni
- 4 cups of shredded mozzarella cheese or any blend you like
- 16 oz. bag of egg noodles cooked & drained as package directs
- 24 oz. of your favourite tomato sauce
- Italian seasonings

Cooking Instructions:

1. Serve 1/3 of the sauce on the bottom of your Ninja, top with noodles (we always stir up this 1st layer of noodles & sauce).

2. Top it with 1/3 of the browned meat. Top again with 1/3 of the cheese & sliced pepperoni & sprinkle on a dash of the seasoning.

3. Repeat layers 2 more times, then set your Ninja to Slow Cook High for about 45 minutes.

4. Now serve hot and enjoy.

Basil Parmesan Chicken, Broccoli & Rice Bake

Preparation time: 20 minutes

Cooking time: 40 minutes

Total time: 60 minutes Serves:

2 to 4 people

Recipe Ingredients:

- 2 large chicken breasts cut in half for 4 servings
- Steak seasoning
- 14 ounces of bag frozen broccoli
- 1 1/3 cups of rice
- 1 can of Progresso Recipe Starter Basil Parmesan
- 1½ cans of water (use the Progresso can)
- ½ cup of shredded cheese of choice to sprinkle on top

Cooking Instructions:

1. Put rice in the pot and stir in the Progresso starter and add 2 cans of water. Add the frozen broccoli and stir adequately.

2. Season chicken breasts with steak seasoning and add to the pot. Set your Ninja on Oven 350°F and cook for about 40 minutes

3. Turn the Ninja off, add the cheese to the top, and return the lid until its ready to eat.

4. Serve and enjoy immediately!

Basil-Tomato Pasta

Preparation time: 10 minutes

Cooking time: 30 minutes

Gross time: 40 minutes

Serve: 2 to 4 people

Recipe Ingredients:

- 12 ounces of linguine pasta
- 15 ounces of can dice tomatoes
- 1 large sweet onion, julienned
- 4 cloves of garlic, thinly sliced
- ½ teaspoon of red pepper flakes
- 2 teaspoons of dried oregano leaves
- 2 large strips of fresh basil chopped
- 4 cups of vegetable broth, plus ½ cup water
- 2 tablespoons of olive oil
- Salt and pepper (to taste)
- Parmesan cheese, for garnish

Cooking Instructions:

1. In the Ninja pot, place pasta, tomatoes, onion, garlic, and basil.

2. Pour in broth and water. Sprinkle the pepper flakes and oregano on top then drizzle with olive oil.

3. Turn Ninja to the Oven setting of 300°F, for 30 minutes. Stir every 5 minutes. A spaghetti serving spoon does well, lifting and stirring gently.

4. Season to taste with salt and pepper. Garnish with Parmesan cheese. It also good with some cooked shrimp, garlic bread.

5. Serve immediately and enjoy!

Beef & Cheese- Better than Hamburger Helper

Preparation time: 10 minutes

Cooking time: 14 minutes

Total time: 24 minutes

Serves: 2 to 4 people

Recipe Ingredients:

- 1 lb. of ground beef
- 1 box of Kraft mac & cheese
- 2 cups of water
- ¼ cup of butter, ¼ cup milk and cheese packet
- Seasonings of preference

Cooking Instructions:

1. Turn the Ninja to Stove Top High. Brown the ground beef. Remove and drain excess grease. Set aside and wipe the Ninja.

2. Add the water and macaroni. Carefully place the lid and turn to 250°F. Set time on Ninja for 10 minutes.

3. Take off the lid and stir for 4 minutes. After Water is evaporated, take the pot out of the Ninja to stop the cooking

4. Now add the beef and season as desired. Add your ¼ cup butter, ¼ cup milk and cheese packet, stir until well mixed.

5. Serve immediately and enjoy.

Beef Nacho Casserole

Preparation time: 10 minutes

Cooking time: 10 minutes

Overall time: 20 minutes

Serves: 2 to 4 people

Recipe Ingredient:

- 1 lb. of ground beef
- 1 can of black beans (drained & rinsed)
- 1 can of sliced black olives (drained)
- 1 to 8 oz. can of tomato sauce
- ¼ cup of salsa
- ¼ tsp. each of garlic salt, cumin & onion powder
- 1 to 2 cups of shredded cheese
- Crushed tortilla chips

Cooking Instructions:

1. Turn your Ninja to Stove mode, select pressure function and set to High pressure to brown the ground beef.

2. Drain any excess grease then turn Ninja to Stove mode and set to cook at Low pressure.

3. Add the tomato sauce and seasonings, let simmer for a few minutes. Add the salsa, beans and olives, top with cheese and tortilla chips.

4. Then turn your Ninja to the Oven setting of 300°F, allow to bake for about 10 minutes.

Broccoli Casserole

Preparation time: 20 minutes

Cooking time: 20 minutes

Overall time: 40 minutes

Serves: 2 to 4 people

Recipe Ingredients:

- 1 cup of cooked rice
- 15 ounces jar of cheese Whiz
- 23 ounces of cream of mushroom soup
- 14 ounces bag of frozen broccoli

Cooking Instructions:

1. Cook the broccoli and rice.

2. Heat up cheese Whiz and soup to the Ninja pot on Stove Top Medium pressure function to melt cheese. Stir frequently.

3. Add broccoli and rice to the Ninja; turn to Oven 350°F and bake for 20 minutes or until boiling. Stir continuously. Then set Ninja to warm mode.

4. Serve and enjoy. It's so good!!

Butter Chicken Curry & Rice

Preparation time: 10 minutes

Cooking time: 25 minutes

Total time: 35 minutes Serves

4 to 6 people

Recipe Ingredients:

- 1 Pound of chicken breasts, cut in small pieces
- 2 tablespoons of butter
- 1 onion, chopped
- Simply Asian seasoning packet
- 15 ounces of tomato sauce
- 2 cups of cooked rice
- ½ cup of light or heavy cream,

Cooking Instructions:

1. Prepare the rice in the Ninja. Remove the rice and wipe out the Ninja.

2. Turn the Ninja to Stove mode and set at High pressure function. Add the chicken to brown. Remove and set aside. Add the butter.

3. Sauté the onions and return the chicken to the Ninja pot. Add the seasoning packet and tomato sauce.

4. Reduce the heat to Stove Top Low-pressure function and simmer for 15 minutes then add the cream. Continue simmering for 10 minutes to thicken the sauce.

5. Enjoy your meal hot.

Fish & Seafood Recipes

Apricot & Country Mustard Salmon

Preparation time: 5 minutes

Cooking time: 10 minutes

Overall time: 15 minutes

Serves: 2 to 4 people

Recipe Ingredients:

- 2 cups of water
- ¼ cup of apricot preserves
- 2 tablespoons of country
- Dijon-style mustard
- 1½ pounds of salmon fillets
- Salt and ground black pepper

Cooking Instructions:

1. Stir preserves to mix up well and mustard in a medium sized bowl. Pour 2 cups of water into pot.

2. Season fish with salt and black pepper. Place fish on roasting rack. Spread preserve mixture on fish; then place rack into pot.

3. Set Ninja to Oven mode of 400°F for 20 minutes (for thick fillets). Check after the period of 10 to 15 minutes for desired doneness.

4. Serve and enjoy.

Cod with Tomato Caper Sauce & Sugar Peas

Preparation time: 5 minutes

Cooking time: 20 minutes

Gross time: 25 minutes

Serves: 2 to 4 people

Recipe Ingredients:

- 2 medium tomatoes, chopped
- ½ cup white wine
- 2 tablespoons drained capers
- 2 cloves garlic, minced
- 1 tablespoon chopped fresh basil leaves
- ½ teaspoon salt
- 4 cod fillets (about 1 pound)
- ¾ pound sugar snap peas

Cooking Instructions:

1. Mix up tomatoes, wine, capers, garlic, basil, and salt in a pot and stir well.

2. Add fish to pot, place snap peas on fish. Set Ninja to Oven mode to 375°F for 10 minutes.

3. Cover and cook until fish flakes are easily when tested with a fork and snap peas are tender-crisp.

4. Serve immediately and enjoy.

Dungeness crab

Preparation time: 10 minutes

Cooking time: 5 minutes

Gross time: 15 minutes Serves:

2 to 4 people

Recipe Ingredients:

- ½ package of penne pasta
- 2 tablespoons of butter
- 2 tablespoon of olive oil
- 2 cloves of garlic, chopped
- 6 sundried tomatoes, sliced thin
- ¾ meat from a fresh cracked crab
- ½ of lemon Juice
- 1 cup of parmesan cheese (divided)

Cooking Instructions:

1. Add pasta to Ninja pot. Cover with about 2 inches of water.

2. Turn Ninja to Stove Top High and boil until desired tenderness. Drain; place in a bowl and set aside.

3. Set Ninja to Stove High pressure and preheat butter and oil in the pot. Now add Garlic and Tomatoes, then stir. Add the crab meat and select Sauté on your Ninja.

4. Stir in the juice from the lemon and ½ cup parmesan cheese. Return the penne to the pot and stir very well. Sprinkle with the remaining parmesan cheese. Gently place the lid.

5. Turn Ninja to Buffet/Warm mode for about 5 minutes, or until penne is warmed through.

6. Now serve and enjoy.

Shrimp & Sausage Pasta

Preparation time: 10 minutes

Cooking time: 20 minutes

Overall time: 30 minutes

Serves: 4 to 6 people

Recipe Ingredients:

- 2 green peppers
- 1 onion
- 1½ pound of shrimp
- 1 package of Italian sausage
- 2 cans of diced tomatoes (we use zesty jalapeño)
- 2 boxes of garlic and olive oil pasta roni

Cooking Instructions:

1. Set Ninja to Stove mode at High pressure; brown peppers, onions and sausage

2. Then add tomatoes. Add the pasta and raw shrimp (you can season with dill, paprika and garlic salt).

3. Set Ninja to Stove function mode and cook at High pressure until it boils. Then set Ninja to Stove Top Low for about 20 minutes.

4. Serve immediately and enjoy!

Shrimp Scampi

Preparation time: 5 minutes

Cooking time: 25 minutes

Overall time: 30 minutes

Serves: 2 to 4 people

Recipe Ingredients:

- 12 ounces of package of frozen shrimp, boiled, peeled and chopped
- 1 pouch of the Campbell's shrimp scampi sauce
- 1 pouch of water
- 2 tbsp. of butter
- 2 tbsp. of minced fresh garlic
- 1 tsp. of onion powder
- a big handful of spinach
- 3 large mushrooms, chopped
- 1 roasted red pepper, chopped
- 1 pound of angel hair noodles

Cooking Instructions:

1. Add all of the ingredients, except the shrimp to the Ninja.

2. Turn Ninja to the Oven mode of 300°F and cook for 20 minutes, stirring frequently. Then add the shrimp the last 5 minutes and stir.

3. Serve and enjoy.

Spicy Mussels

Preparation time: 10 minutes

Cooking time: 30 minutes

Overall time: 40 minutes

Serves: 2 to 4 people

Recipe Ingredients:

- 2 tbsp. of olive oil
- 1 small onion, chopped
- ½ small fennel bulb, chopped (about 2 cups)
- ½ tsp. of salt
- 3 cloves of garlic, minced
- 1 cup of white wine
- 1 cup of vegetable broth
- ½ red pepper (we added more)
- 2 lbs. of mussels, scrubbed
- 1 tbsp. of fresh chopped parsley

Cooking Instructions:

1. Pour oil in crock and set Ninja to Stove Top High; heat up oil.

2. Add onion, fennel and salt to pot. Cook uncovered for 10 minutes or until vegetables are very tender, stirring occasionally.

3. Now, stir in garlic and cook for 1 minute, stirring often. Stir in wine, broth and red pepper.

4. Place mussels on wire rack and place rack into crock. Set Oven to 350°F for 10 minutes.

5. Cover and cook until mussels are tender. Place mussels into serving bowl. Stir parsley into broth mixture and pour broth mixture over mussels.

6. Serve and enjoy!

Tilapia & Tomatoes

Preparation time: 10 minutes

Cooking time: 20 minutes

Overall time: 30 minutes

Serves: 2 to 8 people

Recipe Ingredients:

- 4 to 6 frozen Tilapia
- 2 chopped fresh tomatoes
- Lemon pepper (to taste)
- 1 clove of garlic, minced
- 1 tablespoon of basil
- ½ teaspoon of salt
- 2 cans of cut green beans, drained

Cooking Instructions:

1. Dice tomatoes and sweet peppers. Add garlic, basil, salt, and capers to the pot.

2. Stir gently to mix them up, then add the fish. Set your Ninja to Oven mode at 375°F for about 10 minutes and cover.

3. Place the green beans on top of the fish and set oven to 375°F for another 10 minutes. Cover while cooking.

4. Serve with rice or egg noodles enjoy.

Garlic Parmesan Shrimp with Angel Hair Pasta & Broccoli

Preparation time: 10 minutes

Cooking time: 30 minutes

Overall time: 40 minutes

Serves: 2 to 4 people

Recipe Ingredients:

- 3 cups of water
- 1 box of angel hair pasta
- 2 jars of Ragu Parmesan Garlic Sauce
- 1 bag of frozen chopped broccoli
- Red pepper flakes, to taste
- 1 bag of frozen, already cooked shrimp

Cooking Instructions:

1. Stir ingredients together until well combined, except shrimp. Set Ninja to Oven mode and cook at 325°F for about 15 minutes.

2. Stir again in a bag of frozen, already cooked shrimp and cook for about 3 minutes more.

3. Serve immediately and enjoy!

Low Country Boil

Preparation time: 5 minutes

Cooking time: 30 minutes

Total time: 35 minutes

Serves: 2 to 4 people

Recipe Ingredients:

- 3 cups of water
- 1 package of smoked sausage, sliced
- 6 small corn on the cob
- 5 to 6 red potatoes, quartered
- 1 onion, quartered
- 16 oz. bag of frozen shelled shrimp
- 1 tbsp. of Louisiana concentrated crawfish and shrimp boil*

Cooking instructions:

1. Add all ingredients to your Ninja pot except shrimp. Turn your Ninja to Stove function mode and set to High pressure.

2. Bring to boil and boil for 30 minutes, or until potatoes and onion are tender. Now add the shrimp and cook for more 3 minutes.

3. Serve immediately and enjoy.

Maple Salmon

Preparation time: 5 minutes

Cooking time: 50

Overall time: 55 minutes

Serves: 2 to 4 people

Recipe Ingredients:

- 24 ounces of Salmon
- 5 to 6 tablespoons of real maple syrup
- 3 tablespoons of soy sauce
- clove of garlic
- ¼ teaspoon of garlic salt (We used garlic powder, due to lack of garlic salt)
- 1/8 teaspoon of ground black pepper
- Option pinch of salt since we have no garlic salt

Cooking Instruction:

1. In a small sized bowl, mix up all the ingredients except salmon.

2. Place salmon in shallow baking dish & cover with maple syrup mixture. Cover the dish and marinate salmon in the refrigerator for 30 minutes, turning once.

3. Turn your Ninja to the Oven setting of 400°F. Now add 2 cups of water to the pot. Cover the rack with foil and place the rack in your Ninja.

4. Place the salmon on the rack; cook for 25 minutes or until it easily flakes with a fork. Serve immediately and enjoy!

Panko Parmesan-Crusted Tilapia

Preparation time: 10 minutes

Cooking time: 40 minutes

Overall time: 50 minutes

Serves: 2 to 7 people

Recipe Ingredients:

- ½ cup of seasoned Japanese-style bread crumbs (panko)
- 2 tablespoons of grated parmesan cheese
- ½ teaspoon of paprika
- 1 package (12 ounces) of frozen tilapia fillets 94 fillets)
- 2 tablespoons of Dijon-style mustard

Cooking Instructions:

1. Stir bread crumbs gently, cheese and paprika on plate.

2. Place unwrapped frozen fish into multi-purpose pan, overlapping edges slightly to fit.

3. Brush frozen fish with mustard. Sprinkle with bread crumb mixture. Place pan on rack on top of the pot.

4. Set Oven to 425°F for 40 minutes. Cover and cook until fish flakes easily when tested with fork.

5. Serve and enjoy meal.

Papi's Pepper Garlic Shrimp

Preparation time: 4 minutes

Cooking time: 6 minutes

Total time: 10 minutes

Serves: 2 to 4 people

Recipe Ingredients:

- 1/3 rd. stick of butter
- 6 tbsp. of olive oil
- 5 heaping tablespoons of black pepper
- 4 cubes of frozen garlic cubes
- 1 tbsp. of onion powder
- 1½ lbs. of shrimp
- 2 handfuls of cherry tomatoes

Cooking Instructions:

1. Slowly melt butter then add all other ingredients and allow ingredients (except shrimp and tomatoes) to combine flavours.

2. Turn Ninja to Stove function mode, select and set at High pressure. When Ninja is hot, add shrimp. After 2- or 3-minutes turn shrimp.

3. Add tomatoes and cook for another 3 minutes. Serve immediately and enjoy!

Seafood Linguini

Preparation time: 5 minutes

Cooking time: 25 minutes

Overall time: 30 minutes

Serves: 4 people

Recipe Ingredients:

- 1 pound of bay scallops, the small ones
- 1 pound of shrimp, raw or already cooked
- 1 package crab meat, crumbled
- 2 to 15-ounce cans of white clam sauce
- 1 lb. of linguini
- 26-ounce jars of pasta sauce, your choice of flavour
- 4 cups of water
- Grated cheese, optional

Cooking Instructions:

1. Turn your Ninja to Stove function mode, set at High pressure function and sauté scallops for just a few minutes then add up remaining ingredients.

2. Set your Ninja to Oven mode of 300°F for about 25 minutes. Stir gently and occasionally. When done, sprinkle with grated cheese, if desired.

3. Serve immediately and enjoy.

Shrimp & Crab Boil

Preparation time: 10 minutes

Cooking time: 5 minutes

Gross time: 45 minutes

Serves: 2 to 4 people

Recipe Ingredients:

- McCormick crab & shrimp boil seasoning bag
- 2 Tbsp. of Zatarain's concentrated boil
- 4 cups of water
- 1 quartered onion
- 2 bay leaves
- Garlic cloves
- 2 lemon halves
- Creole seasoning

Cooking Instructions:

1. To the Ninja pot, add all of the ingredients except the Creole seasoning.

2. Turn the Ninja to Stove Top High. Steam cook for 45 minutes. When done, sprinkle some Creole seasoning on the top.

3. Now serve and enjoy!

Salads &Vegetable Recipes
Roasted Brussels Sprouts and Red Radishes

Preparation time: 10 minutes

Cooking time: 20 minutes

Total time: 30 minutes Serves:

2 to 4 people

Recipe Ingredients:

- 1 pound of Brussels sprouts, halved
- ½ pound of red radishes, halved, quartered if large
- 1 tbsp. of olive oil
- Salt and pepper
- ¼ cup of balsamic vinegar, reduced by at least half, until thick

Cooking Instructions:

1. Turn your Ninja to 400°F to preheat while preparing vegetables.

2. Cut sprouts from stem, cut large ones in half, peel stem and cut into similar sized chunks.

3. Toss in large bowl with olive oil and radishes. Stir gently. Roast until leaves are brown and crisp and heads are tender and brown.

4. Radishes will be brown but still slightly crunchy. Remove and plate, sprinkling with balsamic reduction.

5. Serve immediately and enjoy!

Simple Roasted Butternut Squash

Preparation time: 5 minutes

Cooking time: 30 minutes

Gross time: 35 minutes

Serves: 4 to 8 people

Recipe Ingredients:

- 1 to 4 pounds of butternut squash, peeled, seeded and cut into 1-inch cubes
- 3 cloves of garlic with skin
- 2 tablespoons of olive oil
- Salt and pepper

Cooking Directions:

1. Toss squash with oil, garlic, salt and pepper in the Ninja pot. Arrange in single layer.

2. Turn Ninja to the Oven setting of 400°F and roast for about 30 minutes until its tender. Squeeze garlic out of skin and sprinkle over squash.

3. Serve hot or at room temperature and enjoy.

Smothered Cabbage with Pork Chops and Black-Eyed Peas

Preparation time: 5 minutes

Cooking time: 30 minutes

Overall time: 35 minutes

Serves: 4 to 6 people

Recipe Ingredients:

- 2 tablespoons of olive oil
- 1 head of cabbage chopped
- 2 tablespoons of bacon fat
- Salt, pepper, garlic powder, fresh garlic, onion powder, season to taste
- Couple drops of Tabasco sauce
- Pork chops, cut up pieces (amount depending on your family)
- Black eyed peas

Cooking Instructions:

1. Season the Pork on all sides with the seasonings. After that, set Ninja on Stove function mode, set to cook cabbage at Medium pressure.

2. Let it cooks for about 30 minutes. Add the cut-up pieces of pork chops. Now towards the end of cooking, add the black-eyed peas to heat up.

3. Serve immediately and enjoy!

Southern Fried Cabbage

Preparation time: 5 minutes

Cooking time: 10 minutes

Overall time: 15 minutes

Serves: 4 to 6 people

Recipe Ingredients:

- 5 to 6 strips of bacon
- 1 head of cabbage
- 1 tsp. of vinegar
- ¼ tsp. of pepper
- 1 onion diced
- ¼ cup of chicken broth
- ½ tsp. of salt

Cooking Instructions:

1. Turn to Oven mode at 325°F and cook bacon on rack until crispy. Remove bacon and put on paper towel.

2. Place chopped cabbage and onion with bacon grease. Set Ninja to cook medium mode and cook until it begins to wilt.

3. Crumble up bacon and add in pan. Add chicken stock, vinegar, salt, pepper.

4. Then turn your Ninja to Stove Top Low until cabbage is fully cooked stirring frequently.

Southern Style Cabbage with Smoked Turkey Wings with Ninja Corn Bread

Preparation time: 5 minutes

Cooking time: 5 hr. 30 minutes

Overall time: 5 hr. 35 minutes

Serves: 4 to 8 people

Recipe Ingredients:

- 1 Cabbage
- 2 Smoked turkey wings
- 1 Onion chopped
- Chicken broth to the height of wing
- Minced garlic, black pepper, salt

Cooking Instructions:

1. Add turkey wings, Onion, Broth, Garlic, black Pepper, and Salt to the Ninja pot.

2. Turn your Ninja to Slow Cook High pressure mode for 4½ hours. Add the cabbage and continue cooking for 1 hour more.

3. Now serve and enjoy hot.

Spaghetti Squash

Preparation time: 5 minutes

Cooking time: 40 minutes

Gross time: 45 minutes

Serves: 5 to 8 people

Recipe Ingredients:

- Squash
- Garlic
- Italian seasonings
- Turkey sausage
- Parmesan cheese
- Spinach
- Spaghetti sauce

Cooking Instructions:

1. Add 2 cups of water to bottom of Ninja, place rack inside.

2. Cut squash in half, remove seeds, set Ninja to Oven setting of 425°F for 25 minutes.

3. Add the squash spaghetti to the water, add garlic, Italian seasoning, Turkey sausage, parmesan cheese, spinach, and spaghetti sauce

4. Cooked for another 15 minutes. Serve and enjoy!

Stuffed Peppers

Preparation time: 5 minutes

Cooking time: 3 hours

Overall time: 3 hr. 5 minutes

Serves: 2 to 4 people

Recipe Ingredients:

- Left over pork roast, finely chopped
- Cooked kale, finely chopped
- 3 cloves of garlic
- ½ big onion, finely chopped
- 1/3 head of cauliflower, finely chopped
- ¼ cup of Parmesan cheese
- Sprinkled some taco seasoning and pepper flakes
- 1 small can of green chilies enchilada sauce
- 3 green peppers, cleaned and split – (6)

Cooking Instructions:

1. Mix up all the filling ingredients together (except the cheese), and fill the green peppers.

2. Turn your Ninja to cook at slow high-pressure function for 3 hours. Sprinkle with grated cheese. You can put a new spin on that leftover pork roast and kale.

3. Serve immediately and enjoy.

Stuffed Zucchini Boats

Preparation time: 5 minutes

Cooking time: 1 hour 30 minutes

Overall time: 1 hr. 35 minutes

Serves: 2 to 4 people

Recipe Ingredients:

- 1 medium zucchini (reserve seeds)
- 1 lb. very lean hamburger
- ¼ lb. Italian sausage
- ¾ cup of onion, diced
- Salt & pepper to taste (or your favourite seasonings)

Cooking Instructions:

1. Cut the zucchini lengthwise. Using a tablespoon, scoop out the seeds. Mix the hamburger, Sausage, Onion and seeds together.

2. Line the multipurpose pan with foil for easy clean up. Fill the zucchini halves with the meat mixture. Set them into the pan.

3. Add the rack and place the multipurpose pan on your Ninja. Then turn you Ninja to the Oven mode of 350°F. Bake for 1½ hours.

4. Serve with a baked potato.

Taco Pasta Salad

Preparation time: 5 minutes

Cooking time: 1 hour 20 minutes

Gross time: 1 hour 25 minutes

Serves: 2 to 4 people

Recipe Ingredients:

- 1 package of (16 ounces) spiral pasta
- 1 pound of ground beef
- ¾ cup of water
- 1 envelope of taco seasoning
- 2 cups of (8 ounces) shredded cheddar cheese
- 1 large green pepper, chopped
- 1 medium onion, chopped
- 1 medium tomato, chopped
- 2 cans of (2¼ ounces each) sliced ripe olives, drained
- 1 bottle of (16 ounces) Catalina or 16 ounces of Western salad dressing

Cooking Instructions:

1. Cook beef on Ninja Stove top High setting until no longer pink; drain. Add water and taco seasoning; simmer, uncovered for 15 minutes.

2. Cook pasta according to package directions, drain and rinse in cold water, then place in a large bowl.

3. Add beef mixture, cheese, green pepper, onion, tomato and olives; combine thoroughly. Add the dressing and fling to coat.

4. Cover and refrigerate for at least 1 hour.

5. Then, serve and enjoy!

Asparagus with Lemon Aioli

Preparation Time: 5 minutes

Cooking time: 10 minutes

Overall time: 15 minutes

Serves: 1 to 3 people

Recipe Ingredients:

- 1 lemon
- 1/3 cup of light mayonnaise
- 1 small garlic clove, minced
- ¼ teaspoon of salt
- Ground black pepper
- 1 cup of water
- 1 pound of asparagus, trimmed

Cooking Instructions:

1. Grate ½ teaspoon zest and squeeze 2 teaspoons juice from lemon into bowl

2. Stir in mayonnaise, garlic, and salt. Season with black pepper. Pour water into pot. Place roasting rack into pot. Place asparagus on rack.

3. Now set Ninja Oven to 350°F for 10 minutes. Cover and cook until asparagus is tender. Season asparagus with additional salt and black pepper.

4. Serve with lemon aioli and enjoy.

Baked Parmesan Tomatoes

Preparation time: 10 minutes

Cooking time: 15 minutes

Gross time: 25 minutes

Serves: 1 to 3 people

Cooking Ingredients:

- 4 tomatoes, halved horizontally
- ¼ cup freshly grated Parmesan cheese
- 1 teaspoon of chopped fresh oregano
- ¼ teaspoon of salt
- Freshly ground pepper, to taste
- 4 teaspoons of extra-virgin olive oil

Cooking Instructions:

1. Set your Ninja to Oven mode at 425°F and preheat for at least 10 minutes. Place in your Ninja

2. If you have a Pyramid mat use it, or if you have a small baking sheet, place that on top of the pyramid mat. If neither, use your wire rack

3. Top with Parmesan, oregano, salt and pepper. Drizzle with olive oil and bake about 15 minutes or until the tomatoes are tender

4. Now serve to enjoy your meal.

Cabbage Roll Casserole

Preparation time: 10 minutes

Cooking time: 35 minutes

Gross time: 45 minutes

Serves: 1 to 3 people

Recipe Ingredients:

- 2 pounds of ground beef
- 1 cup of chopped onion
- 29 ounces can of tomato sauce
- 3½ pounds of chopped cabbage
- 1 cup of uncooked white rice
- 1 tsp. of salt
- 14 ounces cans beef broth

Cooking Directions:

1. Set your Ninja to Stove Top High-pressure mode and brown your ground beef and onion. If necessary, drain any excess grease.

2. In a large mixing bowl mix up the ingredients; onion, tomato sauce, cabbage, rice and salt.

3. Add meat and mix all together in the crock until well combined. Pour broth over meat mixture and stir. Turn Ninja to Oven setting of 350°F.

4. Place lid carefully. Stir after about every 15 minutes.

Cauliflower Side Dish

Preparation time: 3 minutes

Cooking time: 20 minutes

Total time: 23 minutes

Serves: 6 to 8 people

Recipe Ingredients:

- 1 bag of cauliflower, frozen
- 1 can cream of celery soup
- ½ can of water
- 2 slices of cheddar cheese
- ¼ cup of bread crumbs
- Fresh green beans, (optional)

Cooking Instructions:

1. Add up all the ingredients; the cauliflower, soup, water, cheese and bread crumbs to your Ninja pot.

2. (Fresh green beans from the garden were also added). Turn your Ninja to the Oven setting of 350°F for 20 minutes.

3. Serve immediately enjoy!

Corn Pudding

Preparation time: 5 minutes

Cooking time: 30 minutes

Overall time: 35 minutes

Serves: 2 to 4 people

Recipe Ingredients:

- 2 eggs or ½ cup Egg beaters
- 1 tbsp. of flour
- 2 tbsp. of sugar
- 14 oz. can of whole corn, drained
- 14 oz. can of creamed corn

Cooking Instructions:

1. Mix all ingredients together. Spray Ninja baking pan with butter flavored cooking spray.

2. Pour ingredients into pan. Turn Ninja Oven at 400°F. Then you add 3 cups of water to Ninja pot. Gently put pan on rack. Steam for about 30 minutes.

3. Serve immediately and enjoy.

Craving Beans

Preparation time: 5 minutes

Cooking time: 10 minutes

Gross time: 15 minutes

Serves: 4 to 6 people

Recipe Ingredients:

- 16 to 28 oz. cans of Baked Beans, with liquid
- 15 oz. can of Kidney Beans, with liquid
- 15 oz. can of Butter Beans, with liquid
- 2 to 4 weenies, sliced into small rounds
- 1 onion, chopped
- 1 heaping tablespoon of yellow mustard
- ½ cup of ketchup
- ¾ cup of brown sugar
- ½ tsp. of salt
- ½ tsp. of pepper

Cooking Instructions:

1. Combine all ingredients in your Ninja. Stir gently and continuously until they well combined

2. Turn your Ninja to Slow Cook mode, select pressure function to cook at Low for 7 to 8 hours or select pressure function to cook at High for 3 to 4 hours.

3. After that, cover & cook until thick and bubbly.

4. Serve and enjoy your meal.

Fast & Easy Green Beans

Preparation time: 10 minutes

Cooking time: 40 minutes

Overall time: 50 minutes

Serves: 2 to 4 people

Recipe Ingredients:

- 6 small or 3 large cans of Italian Green Beans (do not drain)
- 1 cup of diced ham (you could use ½ lb. bacon instead)
- 8 to 10 small red potatoes washed & cut into bite size pieces
- 1 teaspoon of salt
- 1 teaspoon of seasoned salt (we used Morton's Season all)
- 1 tablespoon of dried minced onion
- 2 tablespoons of butter

Cooking Instructions:

1. Place all ingredients in the main pot of the Ninja. Stir gently and cook on Stove Top High for 30 minutes.

2. Stir again and reduce to Stove Top Low for another 30 minutes. Switch Ninja to Buffet/Warm mode until ready to serve.

3. Serve and enjoy hot.

Cauliflower Couscous

Preparation time: 15 minutes

Cooking time: 10 minutes

Overall time: 25 minutes

Serves: 4 people

Recipe Ingredients

- 3 cups of cauliflower florets
- 1 clove of garlic, peeled
- 1 tablespoon of fresh rosemary
- ¼ cup plus 2 tablespoons of extra virgin olive oil, divided
- 2 teaspoons of lemon juice
- ½ teaspoon of salt
- ½ teaspoon of ground black pepper
- ½ cup of slivered almonds
- ¼ cup of green onion, sliced

Cooking Instructions

1. Set Ninja to Oven mode and preheat oven to 400°F.

2. Place the cauliflower florets, garlic, and rosemary into the 64-ounce Precision Processor. Then select Chop on Ninja.

3. Toss chopped cauliflower mixture with 2 tablespoons olive oil. Spread evenly on a non-stick baking sheet. Roast for 5 to 7 minutes, then allow to cool slightly.

4. Transfer cauliflower to a mixing bowl. Add remaining ingredients and toss to combine well.

5. Serve immediately and enjoy!

Soup & Stew Recipes

Gazpacho

Preparation time: 20 minutes

Cooking time: 3 hours

Overall time: 3 hr. 20 minutes

Serves: 5 to 8 people

Recipe Ingredients

- ½ small red onion, peeled, cut in quarters
- ½ English cucumber, cut in 2-inch pieces
- ½ green bell pepper, cut in quarters
- ½ red bell pepper, cut in quarters
- 1 lb. of fresh vine-ripe tomatoes, cut in quarters
- ½ jalapeño, seeds removed, cut in quarters
- 2 tbsp. of red wine vinegar
- Juice of 1 lime
- 2 tbsp. of olive oil
- 2 tsp. of salt
- 3 cups of tomato juice

Cooking Instructions:

1. Add all ingredients, except tomato juice, into the 64-ounce Precision Processor in the order listed. Select Chop function button on your Ninja.

2. Add tomato juice and select Cook Low function button on your Ninja for 5 seconds, or until desired consistency is reached.

3. Now serve and enjoy hot.

Roasted Butternut Squash & Apple Soup

Preparation time: 10 minutes

Cooking time: 50 minutes

Overall time: 60 minutes

Serves: 2 to 4 people

Recipe Ingredients

- 2 cups of butternut squash, peeled, cut in 1-inch pieces
- 1 green apple, cut in quarters, sliced
- 2 cloves of garlic, peeled
- 2 tablespoons of olive oil
- 1 tsp. of salt, divided
- ¼ tsp. of paprika
- 2 cups of chicken stock
- Pinch ground black pepper

Cooking Instructions

1. Now preheat Ninja oven to 400°F. Place butternut squash, apple, and garlic onto baking sheet.

2. Drizzle with olive oil and ½ teaspoon salt. Toss to evenly coat. Roast for 40 minutes.

3. Sprinkle with paprika, then place back in oven and roast for another 5 minutes. Carefully remove mixture from oven and let cool for about 15 to 20 minutes.

4. Place the High-Speed Blade into the Jar, then add cooled squash mixture, chicken stock, 1/2 teaspoon salt, and pepper.

5. Pulse 3 times, then run continuously for 60 seconds or until desired consistency is achieved.

6. Transfer soup to medium pot over medium-high heat and cook for 10 minutes, or until heated through.

Zucchini and Summer Squash Soup

Preparation time: 5 minutes

Cooking time: 10 minutes

Total time: 15 minutes

Serves: 2 to 3 people

Recipe Ingredients

- 1 medium white onion, peeled and chopped
- 3 garlic cloves, peeled and minced
- 2 tablespoons of olive oil
- 3 summer squash, sliced
- 3 zucchinis, sliced
- 3 cups of vegetable broth

Cooking Instructions

1. Set Ninja to medium high heat pressure, place the onion, garlic and olive oil into a sauce pot and heat for 5 to 8 minutes or until brown.

2. Add the squash, zucchini and broth and bring to a boil. Once vegetables are tender,

3. Gently remove from heat and allow the mixture to cool. Finally, transfer the mixture to the 40 oz. Blender and blend until it's smooth.

4. Refrigerate and serve chilled.

Kale and Leek Soup

Preparation time: 5 minutes

Cooking time: 25 minutes

Total time: 30 minutes

Serves: 3 to 4 people

Recipe Ingredients

- 2 teaspoons of olive oil
- 1 leek, cleaned and sliced
- 4 cups of kale, chopped and stems removed
- 3 cups of vegetable broth
- Salt and pepper to taste

Cooking Instructions:

1. Heat olive oil in a sauté pan over Ninja medium high heat pressure mode. Add leek and kale and cook until softened and wilted.

2. Add the vegetable broth and cook over medium heat for 20 to 25 minutes or so and then remove from heat.

3. Once cooled, transfer the soup into the 40 oz. Blender and blend until smooth. Microwave or return to pot and heat through.

4. Serve and enjoy.

Strawberry Orange Summer Soup

Preparation time: 5 minutes

Cooking time: 5 minutes

Gross minutes: 10 minutes

Serves 4 to 6 people

Recipe Ingredients:

- 4 cups of strawberries, hulled
- 1 cup of strawberry yogurt
- 1 cup of orange juice
- 2 tablespoons of fresh mint, chopped
- 2 teaspoons of grated orange zest
- 1 teaspoon of agave

Cooking Instructions:

1. Place ingredients into the 72 oz. Ninja Pitcher blend and blend until its smooth.

2. Serve immediately or chill before serving.

Veggie Chowder

Preparation time: 5 minutes

Cooking time: 15 minutes

Gross time: 20 minutes

Serves: 3 to 4 people

Recipe Ingredients

- 1 tablespoon of butter,
- 1 teaspoon of garlic, minced,
- ½ medium white onion, peeled and roughly chopped,
- 2 cups of reduced sodium vegetable broth,
- 2 cups of corn, divided,
- Pinch chili powder,
- Salt and pepper to taste,
- 2 red potatoes, baked and roughly chopped,
- 1 carrot, washed and roughly chopped

Cooking Instructions:

1. Heat butter in a saucepan over Ninja medium heat pressure setting. Add garlic and onion and sauté for 5 minutes.

2. Add broth, 1 cup of corn, chili powder, salt and pepper to taste. Bring to a boil then simmer for 10 minutes.

3. Allow soup to cool, and then transfer to the 48 oz. Pitcher. Add potatoes and pulse 5 to 6 times. Return soup to the saucepan, add carrots and the remaining cup of corn.

4. Turn your Ninja to medium heat mode, cook at medium heat pressure until soup is warmed throughout and vegetables are tender.

5. Serve and enjoy while warm.

Carrot Coriander Soup

Preparation time: 5 minutes

Cooking time: 30 minutes

Gross time: 35 minutes

Serves: 1 to 3 people

Recipe Ingredients:

- ½ lb. of carrots, peeled and roughly chopped,
- ½ small white onion, roughly chopped,
- 1 tbsp. of fresh coriander,
- 2 tbsp. of butter,
- 2 cups of low-sodium chicken broth,
- Salt and pepper to taste,
- Cilantro for garnish

Cooking Instructions:

1. Set your Ninja to the Low Heat pressure mode and melt butter in a large saucepan. Add carrots, onion and coriander, cover and cook for 8 to 10 minutes.

2. Add the broth, salt and pepper, bring to a boil and then cover and simmer for 15 minutes or until carrots are very soft.

3. Allow the soup to cool, and then transfer it into the 40 oz. Blender jar and blend until smooth. Transfer soup back to saucepan and heat until hot.

4. Garnish with cilantro and enjoy!

Sausage & Cabbage Soup

Preparation time: 5 minutes

Cooking time: 10 minutes

Overall time: 15 minutes

Serves: 4 to 6 people

Recipe Ingredients:

- 2 cups of potatoes, peeled and cubed
- 4 cups of shredded cabbage
- 1 carrot shredded, (we bought the pre-shredded and used about ½ the package of 1 large onion)
- 1¼ pounds of sausage
- 4 cups of chicken broth or you can water
- Salt and pepper to taste

Cooking Directions:

1. Place all dry ingredients in your Ninja and pour liquid on top.

2. Cover and set Ninja to cook on Slow Cook at Low pressure function mode for 8 to 10 hours, or High-pressure function mode for 5 hours.

3. Serve immediately and enjoy!

Shipwreck

Preparation time: 5 minutes

Cooking time: 10 minutes

Gross time: 15 minutes

Serves: 2 to 4 people

Recipe Ingredients:

- 1 pound of ground beef
- 1 onion, chopped
- 1 bell pepper or jalapeño - optional
- 2 cans of Campbell's tomato soup. (We use healthy choice)
- 1 soup can, filled with water
- salt and pepper to taste
- 1 can of diced potatoes, drained
- 1 can of kidney beans - (drained)

Cooking Instructions:

1. Turn the Ninja to Stove Top High. Add the beef and onion to brown; also add the bell peppers or jalapeño, if desired. Drain.

2. Add the remaining ingredients and stir gently until they are well combined.

3. Turn the Ninja to Stove to cook at High pressure for 20 minutes. If you would rather have a slow cook meal; turn the Ninja to cook at Slow Low pressure for 4 hours.

4. You can also use the Ninja Oven setting of 350°F for 30 minutes. If choosing the Oven setting, we suggest stirring a few times.

5. Serve and enjoy.

Spicy Beef & Potato Soup

Preparation time: 10 minutes

Cooking time: 50 minutes

Overall time: 60 minutes

Serves: 2 to 4 people

Recipe Ingredients:

- 1 Pounds of hamburger
- 2 teaspoons of salt
- 1 teaspoon of black pepper
- 1 chopped onion
- 4 cups of diced potatoes
- 24 ounces of tomato sauce
- 4 cups of water
- ½ to 1 tablespoon Tabasco – or to taste

Cooking Instructions:

1. Turn your Ninja setting to Stove mode, select pressure function to cook at high pressure to brown the beef.

2. Add the salt, pepper, onions, potatoes, tomato sauce, water and Tabasco sauce.

3. Bring it to a boil. Turn your Ninja to Stove Top Low and cook for an hour, or until the potatoes are fork tender.

4. Serve and enjoy.

Turkey Vegetable Soup

Preparation time: 8 minutes

Cooking time: 8 hours

Overall time: 8 hr. 8 minutes

Serves: 2 to 5 people

Recipe Ingredients

- ½ stick of butter or margarine
- 1 large onion, chopped
- Dark meat turkey, (1-quart Zip-Lock bag from thanksgiving)
- 16 ounces mixed vegetables
- 15 ounces can of corn
- 2 cans of sliced carrots, (drained of liquid)
- 32 ounces of box of chicken broth
- 2 cans of water from the carrots

Cooking Ingredients:

1. Turn the Ninja to Stove Top High pressure mode. Add butter or margarine. Then select Sauté on Ninja and Sauté onion.

2. While the onions are sautéing, chop up the turkey. Add turkey, mixed vegetables, corn, sliced carrots, chicken broth and water to the Ninja pot.

3. Stir continuously until well combined. Turn the Ninja to Slow Cook Low for 8 hours.

4. Soup is ready; serve and enjoy with dinner rolls.

Tuscan White Bean Stew

Preparation time: 5 minutes

Cooking time: 6 hours

Overall time: 6 hr. 5 minutes

Serves: 8 to 10 people

Recipe Ingredients:

- 3 tablespoons. Olive Oil
- 1 medium onion, diced
- 2 Ribs of celery, cut into ½ inch pieces
- 2 Carrots, cut into 1-inch pieces
- 8 cloves of garlic, smashed
- 1 Pound of dried cannellini beans
- 4 cups of chicken broth
- 4 cups of water
- 2 bay leaves
- 2 tsp. of salt
- ½ tsp. of pepper
- Spinach or kale or both
- 1 can of diced tomatoes
- 1 Pound of Kielbasa (purchase pre-cooked and pre-cut into "½" slices).

Cooking Instructions:

1. Turn the Ninja to Stove mode at Medium/High pressure function. Select Sauté on Ninja and Sauté onion, carrots and celery in olive oil until soft.

2. Add the garlic and sauté for a minute more. Add the beans, broth, water, salt and pepper. Stir gently until well combined.

3. Turn the Ninja to Slow Cook Low for 6 hours. After the cook time, add the kielbasa, spinach, kale, (or both), and tomatoes and cook until kale is tender.

4. Remove bay leaves before serving.

Unstuffed Pepper Stew

Preparation time: 5 minutes

Cooking time: 30 minutes

Overall time: 35 minutes

Serves: 4 to 6 people

Recipe Ingredients:

- 2 lbs. of sweet ground Italian sausage
- 1 large sweet onion, cut into slivers
- 2 bell peppers, cut into slivers
- 2 cups of rice
- 2 cups of water
- 24 oz. jar of spaghetti sauce
- 14.5 oz. can of stewed tomatoes
- Cheddar cheese
- Mozzarella cheese
- Italian seasoning
- Garlic powder
- Pepper
- Chives
- Sliced black olives

Cooking Instructions:

1. Turn the Ninja to Stove mode of High pressure. Cook the sausage, onions, and peppers until sausage is cooked through and peppers and onions softened.

2. Add the rice, water, stewed tomatoes and spices. Cover until rice is well cooked.

3. Stir occasionally. Add spaghetti sauce. Stir. Cover for about 5 minutes. Scoop into bowls and sprinkle cheeses, a few black olives and chives.

4. Serve immediately and enjoy your meal. Delicious!

Vegetable Beef Soup

Preparation time: 10 minutes

Cooking time: 6 hours

Overall time: 6 hr. 10 minutes

Serve: 2 to 4 people

Recipe Ingredients:

- 1 beef soup bone
- 4 stalks of celery, cut up
- ½ large onion, chopped
- 32 ounces of box of beef broth
- 15 ounces can of diced tomatoes
- 16 ounces of bag mixed vegetables
- 2 small potatoes, peeled and chopped
- Garlic, salt & pepper (to taste)
- 2 bay leaves
- 1-quart of water
- Spinach (optional)

Cooking Instructions:

1. Add all of the ingredients to the Ninja pot, (except spinach) and turn Ninja to cook at slow cook Low pressure function for 4 to 6 hours.

2. Allow unit to switch to Auto Warm or switch to Buffet setting to hold. Add the spinach at the end if desired.

3. Remove bay leaves before serving.

Nicoise Chicken Stew

Preparation time: 10 minutes

Cooking time: 1 hour 30 minutes

Gross time: 1 hour 40 minutes

Serves: 1 to 3 people

Recipe Ingredients:

- 2 Pounds of chicken pieces
- 10 garlic cloves, peeled
- 25 to 30 nicoise olives
- 28 ounces diced tomatoes
- 2 cups of chicken stock
- 2 tablespoons of fresh rosemary, minced
- 2 tablespoons of fresh thyme, minced
- 2 tablespoons of fresh basil, minced
- 2 tablespoons of fresh parsley, minced
- Cooking fat
- Sea salt and freshly ground black pepper

Cooking Instructions:

1. Turn your Ninja to Stove Top High and select sauté function on the Ninja to sauté your garlic. Remove after sauté.

2. Add your seasoned chicken and brown evenly on all sides. Add the garlic, tomatoes, olives, chicken stock, rosemary, thyme, basil and parsley.

3. Cover and turn your Ninja to 325°F for 1 hours 30 minutes. (We did not use the multipurpose pan. It's directly in the Ninja pot.)

4. But if you have time, you can add everything and set Ninja to cook on slow cook pressure for 2 to 4 hours.

5. Test the chicken with a digital thermometer and add more time if necessary.

6. Serve and enjoy.

Chicken Stew

Preparation time: 5 minutes

Cooking time: 6 hours

Overall time: 6 hours 5 minutes

Serves: 2 to 4 people

Recipe Ingredients:

- 4 chicken breasts cut in cubes
- 3 to 4 potatoes, diced
- 2 to 3 stalks celery, diced
- 3 to 4 carrots, diced
- 2 cans (10 ounces, each) of cream of chicken soup
- 1 chicken of bouillon cube
- 2 tsp. of garlic salt
- 1 tsp. pepper
- 16-ounce bag frozen mixed vegetables

Cooking Instructions:

1. Add cubed chicken and fresh vegetables to your Ninja. Pour soup overall and add seasonings

2. Turn Ninja to Slow Cook High and cook for 4 to 5 hours. Add the frozen vegetables and continue cooking for 1 more hour

3. Let the unit go to Auto Warm or turn it to Buffet setting to hold until ready to eat.

4. Serve immediately and enjoy!

Baked Beef Stew

Preparation time: 5 minutes

Cooking time: 45 minutes

Overall time: 50 Minutes

Serves: 3 to 5 people

Recipe Ingredients:

- 2 packages stew meat cut into small pieces
- 4 large potatoes diced
- ½ package baby carrots (or small bag)
- 1 onion diced
- 1 can of tomato soup
- 1 can of water
- 2 tablespoon of tapioca (minute)
- 2 Tablespoon of Worcestershire Sauce
- Salt and pepper

Cooking Instructions:

1. Use all the above ingredients and layer in the Ninja.

2. Set Ninja to oven mode of 300°F and bake for about 45 minutes. After 45 minutes.

3. Serve immediately and enjoy!

Beef Stew

Preparation time: 5 minutes

Cooking time: 7 hours

Overall time: 7 hr. 5 minutes

Serves: 2 to 4 people

Recipe Ingredients:

- 1 can (10 ¾ oz.) of tomato soup, undiluted
- 1 cup of water or red wine
- ¼ cup of flour
- 2 lbs. of beef cubes
- 3 carrots, cut in 1-inch slices
- Onions, to your liking
- 4 medium potatoes, cut in 1½ inch chunks
- ½ cup celery, cut in chunks
- 12 whole large mushrooms, optional
- 2 beef of bouillon cubes
- 1 tbsp. Italian Herb mix seasoning or 1 teaspoon each: oregano, thyme and rosemary; or parsley flakes, oregano, & thyme
- Salt & pepper, to taste

Cooking Instructions:

1. Mix together the soup, water or wine and flour until smooth. Add remaining ingredients to your Ninja.

2. Turn Ninja to Slow Cook mode and cook at Low pressure for about 6 to 7 hours.

3. Serve over wide noodles with some French or Italian bread.

Thai Chicken Coconut Curry Soup

Preparation time: 5 minutes

Cooking time: 30 minutes

Total time: 35 minutes

Serves: 2 to 4 people

Recipe Ingredients

- 3 cups of coconut milk, filtered, from a carton
- 2 tablespoons of vegetable oil
- 3 cloves of garlic, peeled
- 1 white onion, diced
- 3 cups of chicken broth
- 3 tablespoons of red curry paste
- 3 tablespoons of soy sauce
- 3 tablespoons of lime juice
- 1 tablespoon of brown sugar
- 1 tablespoon of ground turmeric
- 2 boneless chicken breasts, cut into 2-inch strips
- 4 cups of rice stick noodles or vermicelli, cooked
- 1 cup of bean sprouts
- Lime wedges, for garnish
- Cilantro leaves, chopped

Cooking Instructions

1. Heat oil in a stockpot and sauté garlic and onion on Ninja medium heat setting until softened, about 10 minutes. Cool to room temperature.

2. Using the Bottom Blades in the Pitcher, add the cooled vegetables, coconut milk, chicken broth, curry paste, soy sauce, lime juice, brown sugar and turmeric.

3. Select Speed 1 and flip the switch to Start. Slowly increase to Speed 6 and blend until smooth.

4. Return mixture to the stockpot, add chicken and bring to a boil. Reduce heat and simmer for about 10 minutes, or until chicken is cooked through with no pink.

5. To serve, divide noodles between bowls, ladle soup and garnish each serving with bean sprouts, a lime and chopped cilantro.

Appetizer, Snacks, Sauce & Side Dishes

Thai Chili Chicken Wings

Preparation time: 10 minutes

Cooking time: 30 minutes

Overall time: 40 minutes

Serves: 2 to 4 people

Recipe Ingredients

- ½ of cup water
- 2 pounds of frozen chicken wings, drums and flats separated
- 2 tablespoons of canola oil
- 2 tablespoons of Thai chili sauce
- 2 teaspoons of kosher salt
- 2 teaspoons of sesame seeds, for garnish

Cooking Instructions

1. Pour water into Ninja pot. Place wings into the Cook & Crisp™ Basket and place basket in pot.

2. Assemble the pressure lid, making sure the pressure release valve is in the seal position.

3. On Ninja Menu Select Pressure and set to High pressure. Set time to 12 minutes. Select Start/Stop to begin.

4. When pressure cooking is complete, quickly release the pressure by moving the pressure release valve to the Vent position.

5. Carefully remove lid when unit has finished releasing pressure. Pat wings dry with paper towels and toss with 2 tablespoons oil in the basket.

6. Close the crisping lid. Select Air Crisp, set temperature to 390°F, and set time to 15 minutes. Select Start/Stop to begin.

7. After 7 minutes, open lid, then lift basket and shake wings or toss them with silicone-tipped tongs. Lower basket back into pot and close lid to resume cooking.

8. While the wings are cooking, stir together Thai chili sauce and salt in a large mixing bowl.

9. When cooking is complete, transfer wings to the bowl with chili sauce and toss to coat.

10. Garnish with sesame seeds and serve.

Chai Peanut Butter

Preparation time: 10 minutes

Cooking time: 20 minutes

Overall time: 30 minutes

Serves: 1 to 3 people

Recipe Ingredients

- 3 cups of unsalted roasted peanuts, divided
- 1 tablespoon of maple syrup
- 1 tablespoon of ground cinnamon
- 1/2 teaspoon of ground cardamom
- ¼ teaspoon of ground ginger
- ¼ teaspoon of ground cloves
- ¾ teaspoon of kosher salt
- 2 tablespoons of vegetable oil

Cooking Instructions

1. Place 1½ cups roasted peanuts, maple syrup, cinnamon, cardamom, ginger, cloves, salt, and oil into the Pitcher.

2. Place remaining peanuts on top. Turn dial to Nut Butter, then press start/stop button to begin. While program is running.

3. If necessary, you can carefully remove the lid cap and use the tamper to push ingredients from the sides of the Pitcher toward the blades.

4. Store in an airtight container in the refrigerator.

Beef Jerky

Preparation time: 15 minutes

Cooking time: 5 hours

Overall time: 5 hr. 15 minutes

Serves: 4 to 6 people

Recipe Ingredients

- ¼ cup of soy sauce
- 2 tablespoons of Worcestershire sauce
- 2 tablespoons of dark brown sugar
- 1 teaspoon of ground black pepper
- 1 teaspoon of garlic powder
- 1 teaspoon of onion powder
- 1 teaspoon of paprika
- 2 teaspoons of kosher salt
- 1-pound uncooked beef eye of round, cut in ¼ -inch slices

Cooking Instructions

1. Whisk together all ingredients, except beef. Place mixture into large resalable plastic bag. Add beef to bag and rub to coat.

2. Marinate in refrigerator for 8 hours or overnight. Strain meat; discard excess marinade. Remove the crisper plate from the basket.

3. Lay half the sliced meat flat on the bottom of the basket in one layer. Place the crisper plate on top of the meat. Place remaining meat on the crisper plate.

4. Insert basket in unit. In your Ninja, Select Dehydrate, set temperature to 150°F, and set time to 7 hours.

5. Select Start/Pause function button to begin. Check after 5 hours, then cook until desired texture is reached.

6. When cooking is complete, remove jerky and store in an airtight container.

Boiled Peanuts

Preparation time: 30 minutes

Cooking time: 13 hr. 30 minutes

Overall time: 14 hr. 30 minutes

Serves: 1 to 3 people

Recipe Ingredients:

- 12 cups of water
- 2 pounds of raw peanuts
- ½ cup salt

Cooking Instructions:

1. Rinse peanuts until water runs clear. Put all ingredients in the Ninja and give it a good and frequent stir until all ingredients are well combined

2. Cover and cook on Slow Cook mode at High pressure function for about 12 to 14 hours or until done to your liking.

3. Check them every few hours, give them a good stir and add water as needed.

4. Once it's done and tender serve and enjoy.

Party Meatballs

Preparation time: 30 minutes

Cooking time: 4 hours

Overall time: 4 hr. 30 minutes

Serves: 2 to 4 people

Recipe Ingredients:

- 1 to 28- oz. bag of frozen meatballs
- 1 to 18-oz. jar of grape jelly
- 1 to 12-oz. jar of chili sauce (use about 6 ounces)
- 1 to 18-oz. bottle of BBQ sauce
- 1 large Vidalia onion, chopped

Cooking Directions:

1. Chop or mince onion to desired-sized pieces. Place chopped onion on the bottom of your Ninja pot.

2. Stir together grape jelly, BBQ sauce, and chili sauce in separate bowl until thoroughly blended.

3. Add sauce to the Ninja pot and combine with onions until well blended. Add meatballs to the Ninja and stir until meatballs are coated.

4. Cook the meatballs in sauce for 4 to 5 hours on Slow Cook mode at Low pressure or 2 to 2½ hours on Slow Cook at High pressures until meatballs are cooked through. Stir occasionally.

5. Serve and enjoy.

Popcorn

Preparation time: 5 minutes

Cooking time: 15 minutes

Total time: 20 minutes

Serves: 2 to 4 people

Recipe Ingredients:

- 3 tablespoons of cooking oil
- ½ cup of popcorn

Cooking Instructions:

1. Turn your Ninja to Stove mode, set to pressure function to cook at High pressure. Add oil and use paper towel to even out oil

2. Couple un-popped kernels and cover. Once the kernels stop popping, add the rest right away.

3. Tilt Ninja for a couple of times while it's still cooking just to be sure oil was spreading evenly.

4. When you hear popping slowing down that means it's about done. Just salt/season/butter to taste.

5. Serve immediately and enjoy.

Roasted Garbanzo Beans

Preparation time: 7 minutes

Cooking time: 1 hour

Total time: 1 hr. 7 minutes

Recipe Ingredients:

- 1 can of Garbanzo beans, drained and towel dried
- 1 tsp. of olive oil
- Seasonings of choice (we used Cajun)

Cooking Instructions:

1. First of all, dry the beans, put them in a quart zip lock, poured in the oil, season and toss them.

2. Make use of Ninja cake pan, placed the beans in a single layer, set pan on the rack.

3. Set Ninja to Oven setting at 350°F for 1 hour! Stir once or twice during baking.

4. Serve immediately and enjoy.

Cinnamon Pecans

Preparation time: 30 minutes

Cooking time: 4 hours

Overall time: 4 hr. 30 minutes

Serves: 2 to 4 people

Recipe Ingredients:

- 4 cups of pecan halves
- 1 cup of sugar
- 1 cup of brown sugar
- 3 egg whites
- 2½ teaspoons of vanilla
- 3 tablespoons of cinnamon

Cooking Instructions:

1. In a medium sized bowl, whip egg whites and vanilla until frothy. Add pecans to the egg mixture and toss to coat.

2. Add sugar, brown sugar and cinnamon and toss. Add pecans to your greased Ninja pot. Turn Ninja to Slow Cook at Low pressure function for 3½ hours.

3. After they are done, add 3 tablespoons of water and stir gently. Place pecans on a lightly greased cookie sheet to cool for 1 hour.

4. When pecans is ready, store in an airtight container.

Sweet Potato Curly Fries

Preparation time: 15 minutes

Cooking time: 40 minutes

Gross time: 55 minutes

Serves: 2 to 4 people

Recipe Ingredients

- 3 medium sweet potatoes, peeled, trimmed
- 2 tablespoons of canola oil
- 2 teaspoons of salt
- 1 teaspoon of ground black pepper
- Honey Mustard Sauce
- ½ cup of Dijon mustard
- ½ cup of honey

- 2 tablespoons of mayonnaise
- 1 tablespoon of lemon juice
- ¼ teaspoon of salt
- ½ teaspoon of ground black pepper

Cooking Instructions:

1. Set Ninja to Oven mode and preheat oven at 400°F. Line a baking sheet with parchment paper and coat with cooking spray; set aside.

2. Place all Honey Mustard Sauce ingredients in a bowl and whisk until well combined; set aside.

3. Position Spaghetti Blade onto Collecting Bowl and assemble Feed Chute Lid. Place sweet potato into feed chute; secure on Blade Disc pin.

4. Firmly secure pusher. Select start/Stop; process sweet potato. Transfer sweet Potato Noodles to a medium size mixing bowl and set aside.

5. Repeat process with second and third sweet potatoes. Then toss sweet potato noodles with oil, salt, and pepper.

6. Evenly distribute on prepared baking sheet. Bake for about 40 to 45 minutes, tossing gently every 15 minutes, until golden brown.

7. Serve and enjoy immediately.

Carrot Hummus

Preparation time: 30 minutes

Cooking time: 20 minutes

Overall time: 50 minutes

Serves: 5 to 8 people

Recipe Ingredients:

- 2 cups of carrots, peeled, cut in 1-inch pieces
- 3 cloves of garlic, peeled
- ¼ cup of extra virgin olive oil
- 1 ½ tsp. of kosher salt, divided
- 1 cup of canned chickpeas, drained
- ½ cup of vegetable stock
- ¼ cup of fresh lemon juice
- ½ tsp. of cayenne pepper
- 1 tsp. of paprika

Cooking Instructions

1. Preheat oven to 425°F. Place carrots and garlic in a bowl and toss with olive oil and ½ teaspoon salt.

2. Set Ninja to Oven mode and roast for 20 minutes. Remove from oven and let cool 20 minutes.

3. Place the High-Speed Blade into the Jar, then add all ingredients in the order listed.

4. Pulse 6 to 10 times, then run continuously for 60 seconds, or until ingredients are well combined.

5. Serve hummus with Pita Bread.

Broccoli Tots

Preparation time: 20 minutes

Cook time: 30 minutes

Overall time: 50 minutes

Serves: 2 to 4 people

Recipe Ingredients:

- 2 ½ cups of broccoli, cut in 1¼ inch florets
- ¼ small onion, cut in 1¼-inch pieces
- 1 large egg
- 2/3 cup of panko bread crumbs
- ¼ teaspoon of salt
- ¼ teaspoon of ground black pepper
- ½ cup of shredded cheddar cheese for a mild flavour OR
- ½ cup of shredded pepper jack cheese for a spicy, peppery flavour.

Recipe Instructions:

1. Set Ninja to Oven mode and preheat at 400°F. Line a baking pan with parchment paper and coat with cooking spray, set aside.

2. In a medium saucepan, bring 1-quart water to a boil. Blanch broccoli for 1 minute. Remove broccoli and immediately plunge into ice water. Drain well.

3. Place cooled broccoli and onion into the Nutri Bowl. On you Ninja, select AutoiQ Boost No Fusion Chop.

4. Transfer mixture into a medium mixing bowl. Add egg, cheese, bread crumbs, salt, and pepper and mix thoroughly.

5. Shape mixture into 24 cylinders about ¾ inch wide by 1-inch long. Place on prepared baking pan and bake for 25 minutes, or until tots are crispy, gently flipping halfway through.

6. Serve immediately and enjoy.

Chicken and Apple Sausage

Preparation time: 10 minutes

Cooking time: 15 minutes

Overall time: 25 minutes

Serves: 5 to 8 people

Recipe Ingredients

- 1 small onion, peeled, quartered
- 2 apples, peeled, cored, quartered
- 1/3 cup of fresh sage leaves
- 1 tbsp. of olive oil
- 1 lb. of uncooked boneless, skinless chicken thighs, cut in 2-inch cubes
- Pinch of cinnamon
- ¾ tsp. of kosher salt
- ¾ tsp. of fresh ground pepper

Cooking Instructions:

1. Preheat oven at 350 °F. Line a baking sheet with parchment paper; set aside.

2. Place the onion, apples, and sage into the 40-ounce Processor Bowl. Pulse, using short pulses, until finely chopped, about 5 times.

3. Heat the olive oil in a medium skillet over medium heat pressure. Add the onion, the apple mixture and sauté 3 to 5 minutes, until soft.

4. Remove from heat and place in a large bowl. Place the cubed chicken into the 40-ounce Processor Bowl. Pulse, 6 to 8 times using long pulses, until finely ground.

5. Add the ground chicken to the bowl with the onion and apple mixture. Add the cinnamon and season with salt and pepper. Mix well, using your hands.

6. Form mixture into 8 patties and bake on a parchment line cookie sheet for about 10 to 12 minutes, or until fully cooked.

Ketogenic Recipes

Low Carb Beef and Sausage Alfredo

Preparation time: 10 minutes

Cooking time: 15 minutes

Overall time: 25 minutes

Recipe Ingredients:

- 1 lb. of lean hamburger
- 1 lb. of spicy sausage
- 1 bag of frozen broccoli (cook in micro for about 3 minutes)
- 2 to 24 oz. jars of Alfredo sauce
- 1 cup of shredded cheese
- Garlic salt and black pepper – to taste

Cooking Instructions:

1. Set your Ninja to Stove mode function, preheat at High pressure and brown hamburger and sausage, with garlic salt and pepper. Drain afterwards.

2. Add broccoli and Alfredo sauce, stir gently until well combined. Turn your Ninja to the Oven setting of 350°F and cook for about 10 minutes.

3. Turn off your Ninja. Add shredded cheese on top. Let it rest for a few minutes.

4. Serve immediately and enjoy.

Italian Meatballs & Cabbage

Preparation time: 10 minutes

Cooking time: 6 hours

Overall time: 6 hr. 10 minutes

Recipe Ingredients:

- 2 pounds of Jimmy Dean roll sausage
- Eggs
- 2 ounces of grated parmesan cheese
- 2 tbsp. of Italian herbs
- Large onion, cut in slices, not diced
- Cabbage, cut into ½" slices
- 1 can of green beans, drained
- 1 can of Italian diced tomatoes

Cooking Instructions:

1. In a medium size mixing bowl, mix sausage with an egg, parmesan cheese, and Italian herbs. Form into "1½" meatballs and set aside.

2. Add the onion to the bottom of the Ninja pot. Add ½ slices of cabbage till the onion is covered. Add the meatballs on top of the cabbage, spreading out evenly.

3. Add the green beans and diced tomatoes and spread evenly. That's it. Cook in the Ninja for 6 hours on Slow Cook mode at Low pressure.

4. If you like garlic, add in a few chopped up cloves before cooking.

5. Serve and enjoy.

Frittata – Low Carb

Preparation time: 5 minutes

Cooking time: 10 minutes

Overall time: 15 minutes

Serves: 1 to 3 people

Recipe Ingredients:

- 1 tbsp. of butter
- 3 eggs
- 1/3 cup of heavy cream
- Salt and freshly ground pepper - to taste
- Sharp cheddar cheese - shredded
- 6 to 8 pepperoni slices

Cooking Instructions:

1. Start by setting your Ninja to Stove mode to cook at High pressure. Add butter to melt. Sauté the vegetables until tender.

2. Then blend the eggs with the heavy cream. Turn the Ninja to the dry Oven setting of 325°F.

3. Pour the egg mixture evenly over the vegetables, cooking for about 5 minutes.

4. Adding salt and freshly ground pepper to taste. When eggs are set, top with sharp cheddar cheese and pepperoni.

5. Carefully cover with the lid and let the remaining heat melt the cheese.

6. Serve and enjoy hot.

Cheeseburger Soup

Preparation time: 10 minutes

Cooking time: 20 minutes

Gross time: 30 minutes

Serves: 1 to 3 people

Recipe Ingredients:

- 1-pound of ground turkey
- 2 teaspoon of onion powder
- 1 teaspoon of basil
- 3 cups of chicken broth
- 1 cup each of frozen broccoli, cauliflower
- ½ cup of frozen carrots
- 1½ cups of fat free half and half
- 8 ounces of shredded cheddar cheese
- 1 cup of onion, chopped
- 4 cloves of garlic, minced

Cooking Instructions:

1. Turn the Ninja to the Oven setting of 425°F. Brown ground turkey and drain off any fat.

2. Return to Ninja and add onion powder, onions, and garlic. Brown a little longer to flavour the meat. Add chicken broth, basil and frozen veggies.

3. Bring to boil and turn the Ninja down to Stove Top Low. Cover and cook about 20 minutes, or until the veggies are tender.

4. Add in half and half and then the shredded cheese. Turn off heat and stir gently until cheese is melted.

5. Serve hot and enjoy.

Chicken & Vegetables

Pepperoni Pizza Chicken

Preparation time: 5 minutes

Cooking time: 35 minutes

Gross time: 40 minutes

Serves: 4 to 8 people

Recipe Ingredients:

- 8 chicken breasts, pounded out a bit
- 1 small jar of pizza sauce
- 1 cup of shredded cheese
- 1 package of pepperoni (We used the smaller spicy hot)
- 1 can of olives, sliced
- Salt
- Pepper
- Italian seasoning
- Oregano
- Olive oil

Cooking Instructions:

1. Turn the Ninja to Stove mode and set to cook at High pressure.

2. Season one side of the Chicken. Add olive oil to the pot and add the Chicken, placing the seasoned side down.

3. Season other side of chicken. Brown Chicken for about 5 minutes on each side or until it's cooked through.

4. Add the sauce, cheese, pepperoni and olives. Turn the Ninja to Stove mode to cook at Low pressure. Gently place the lid and cook for 30 minutes.

5. Serve in bowls as it's a bit saucy and yum! Delicious!!!

Meatballs with Spinach, Mushrooms & Sauce

Preparation time: 5 minutes

Cooking time: 3 hours

Total time: 3 hours 5 minutes

Serves: 3 to 5 people

Recipe Ingredients:

- 10 oz. of chopped spinach
- 16 oz. of meatballs
- 24 oz. of jar sauce
- 2 tbsp. of minced garlic
- 8 oz. of sliced mushrooms
- ½ cup of diced onion
- 1 tbsp. of olive oil
- Angel pasta (optional)
- Parmesan cheese for topping

Cooking Instructions:

1. Turn the Ninja to Stove Top High. Heat the olive oil. Add the meatballs to brown and the onions and mushrooms to sauté.

2. When done, add the sauce and spinach. Turn Ninja to Slow Cook Low for 3 hours. Stirring gently a couple of times.

3. This is a Low Carb recipe. It can be used as an appetizer or with your favorite pasta. Serve and enjoy.

No Bun Cheeseburger

Preparation time: 5 minutes

Cooking time: 6 minutes

Total time: 11 minutes Serves:

2 to 4 people

Recipe Ingredients:

- 2/3-pound of 85/15 lean beef
- 1/3 cup chopped Vidalia onion
- ¼ tsp. minced garlic
- ½ tsp. of crushed red pepper
- 2 slices of American cheese

Cooking Instructions:

1. Combine all ingredients except cheese slices and make two patties.

2. Set Ninja on Stove mode to cook at High pressure, cook burgers until tender for 6 minutes on each side.

3. Place patties on plate and add cheese slices. Serve and enjoy.

No Carb Delicious Meatballs

Preparation time: 10 minutes

Cooking time: 40 minutes

Total time: 50 minutes

Serves: 4 to 6 people

Recipe Ingredients:

- ½ Pound of each: ground pork, ground sirloin, ground veal • 2 eggs
- ½ cup of shredded Parmesan cheese
- ¼ cup of stone ground Mustard
- ¼ cup of hot Sauce
- 2 tablespoons of minced garlic
- ½ teaspoon of salt
- ¼ teaspoon of pepper

Cooking Instructions:

1. Mix all ingredients together and form golf ball size meatballs.

2. Brown the meatballs on Stove Top High, then turn Ninja to Oven at 375°F for 25 minutes.

3. Next remove the meatballs & place on rack. (They are okay to touch, but try to keep it in single layer.)

4. Place the rack into the Ninja and carefully cover with lid. The meatballs will be ready in 20 minutes.

5. Note: the mustard and hot sauce are optional, but are included in this recipe because they really flavour, moisten, and tenderize the meatballs well.

Zucchini Casserole, Low Carb

Preparation time: 5 minutes

Cooking time: 20 minutes

Total time: 30 minutes

Serves: 6 to 8 persons

Recipe Ingredients:

- 1½ lbs. of zucchini
- 1 small onion
- 2 tbsp. of butter
- 1 cup (4 oz.) of diced green chilies
- 3 tbsp. of flour
- ½ tsp. of salt
- ¼ tsp. of pepper
- 1½ cups of jack cheese
- 1 egg
- 1 cup of small curd cottage cheese • 2 tbsp. of minced parsley
- ½ cup of grated parmesan cheese

Cooking Instructions:

1. Dice Zucchini. Combine with onion and butter in Ninja on Stove Top Medium pressure mode. Sauté.

2. Mix in drained chilies, flour, salt and Pepper. Sprinkle with jack cheese. Also, mix egg with cottage cheese and parsley and spoon over the top.

3. Sprinkle with parmesan cheese. After that, set Ninja to oven mode and bake at 300°F for 20 minutes, or until center becomes hot.

4. Serve immediately and enjoy.

Chicken Breasts with Spinach-Feta

Preparation time: 10 minutes

Cooking time: 20 minutes

Overall time: 30 minutes

Serves: 4 to 8 people

Recipe Ingredients:

- Spinach
- Feta Cheese
- Salt and pepper
- Paprika
- Chicken Breasts
- Mozzarella cheese

Cooking Instructions:

1. Cook spinach in saucepan, season with salt and pepper and add feta cheese to the mixture.

2. Season chicken breasts with salt, pepper, and paprika. Place in the Ninja. Top chicken breasts with spinach-feta mixture.

3. Add mozzarella cheese to cover it up. After that, turn Ninja to Oven Setting at 350°F and cook for 30 minutes.

4. Healthy and delicious!

Dessert Recipes

5 Ingredients Pumpkin Cake

Preparation time: 10 minutes

Cooking time: 50 minutes

Total time: 60 minutes

Serves: 8 to 10 people

Recipe Ingredients:

- 1 yellow cake mix
- 1 tablespoon of pumpkin pie spice
- 1 can of pumpkin
- 1 Cup dried cranberries
- ½ Bag of dark chocolate chips

Cooking Instructions:

1. Mix all ingredients together until well combined. Add the batter to the Ninja multipurpose pan. Gently place on the rack.

2. Now turn your Ninja Oven setting to 350°F. Do not add water. Bake for about 50 minutes.

3. Ready for consumption, enjoy!

Apple Cobbler

Preparation time: 10 minutes

Cooking time: 25 minutes

Overall time: 35 minutes

Serve: 2 to 4 people

Recipe Ingredients:

- 2 cups of apples, diced
- 2 cups of milk
- 2 cups of sugar
- 2 cups of flour
- 2 tablespoons of butter, melted
- A little cinnamon and vanilla

Cooking Instructions

1. Mix together all ingredients until well combined, (except apples) and pour into the multipurpose pan. Push apples into the mixture.

2. Turn the Ninja to Oven setting, of 350°F for 25 minutes. Serve immediately and enjoy hot.

Apple Crumble

Preparation time: 30 minutes

Cooking time: 2 hours

Overall time: 2 hrs. 30 minutes

Serves: 4 to 6 people

Recipe Ingredients:

- 4 apples, peeled and chopped
- 1 cup of brown sugar
- 1 tablespoon of flour
- 1 teaspoon of cinnamon
- Crumble
- 1 cup of flour
- 1 cup of oats
- 1 cup of brown sugar
- ½ cup of butter
- 1 teaspoon of cinnamon
- Dark chocolate sprinkles

Cooking Instructions:

1. Mix together the apples, brown sugar, flour, and cinnamon. Add to the Ninja pot.

2. Mix the crumble and sprinkle on top. Then turn the Ninja to Slow Cook mode to cook at High pressure for 2 hours.

3. After 2 hours Apple Crumble is ready.

Macchiato Cupcakes

Preparation time: 10 minutes

Cooking time: 20 minutes

Gross time: 30 minutes

Serves: 2 to 4 people

Recipe Ingredients:

- White cake mix
- ¾ cup 1% buttermilk
- 2 tsp. of pure coffee extract
- 1 can of Duncan Hines cream cheese frosting, (or your favourite brand)
- 2 tsp. of pure coffee extract

Cooking Instructions:

1. Mix all together until well combined. Place 2 cups of water into the pot. Place the rack and the cupcakes.

2. Turn Ninja to oven mode and steam bake at 350°F for 25 minutes and Cool.

3. Add 2 teaspoon of pure coffee extract to the can of Duncan Hines cream cheese frosting (or your favourite brand), and stir to mix. Frost.

4. Serve and enjoy.

Cherry Dump Cake

Preparation time: 10 minutes

Cooking time: 30 minutes

Overall time: 40 minutes

Serves: 4 to 8 people

Recipe Ingredients:

- 1 can of (21 oz.) cherry pie filling or any kind of fruit
- 1 box yellow or butter cake mix
- 1 stick salted butter

Cooking Instructions:

1. Spray the Ninja pot with Pam. Pour in the pie filling. Sprinkle the cake mix evenly across the top.

2. Add with butter pats across the mixture. Turn to the Oven setting of 275°F for about 35 minutes or until brown on top.

3. Now serve and enjoy, delicious!

Chocolate Lava Cake

Preparation time: 30 minutes

Cooking time: 2 hours 30 minutes

Overall time: 3 hours

Serves: 2 to 4 people

Recipe Ingredients:

- Cake:
- 1 box Betty Crocker™ Super Moist™ triple chocolate fudge cake mix
- 1¼ cups of milk
- ½ cup of vegetable oil
- 3 eggs • Topping:
- 1 box of (4-serving size) instant chocolate pudding and pie filling mix
- 2 cups of milk
- 1 bag of (12 oz.) milk chocolate chips (2 cups)

Cooking Instructions:

1. Spray the Ninja with a cooking spray. In large mixing bowl, beat cake ingredients with electric mixer as directed on cake mix box. Pour into the Ninja pot.

2. In a medium mixing bowl, beat pudding mix and 2 cups milk with whisk as directed on box.

3. Pour into Ninja over the cake butter. Do not mix. Sprinkle chocolate chips over top.

4. Place the lid. Cook on Slow Cook Low for 2 hrs. 30 minutes to 3 hours or until cake is set and pudding is beginning to bubble out of cake.

5. Serve and enjoy.

Dump Cake

Preparation time: 30 minutes

Cooking time: 1 hours 30 minutes

Overall time: 2 hours

Serves: 8 to 10 people

Recipe Ingredients:

- 1 box yellow cake mix
- 1 can of Apple pie filing (or any flavor like blueberry too)
- 1 stick of real butter

Cooking Instructions:

1. Put pie filling in bottom of Ninja and sprinkle box of cake mix on top. Slice butter into pats and place on top of cake mix.

2. Then set Ninja to Slow Cook at High pressure for 2 hours. After the period of 2 hours serve warm with ice cream.

Maple Pumpkin Flan

Preparation time: 30 minutes

Cooking time: 3 hours 30 minutes

Overall time: 4 hours

Serves: 2 to 4 people

Recipe Ingredients:

- ½ cup of pure maple syrup
- 3 eggs
- ¾ cup of canned pumpkin
- ½ cup of milk
- ¼ cup of sugar
- 1 tsp. of pumpkin pie spice
- 1 tsp. of vanilla extract
- 8 cups of water

Cooking Instruction:

1. Place 2 tablespoon syrup in four (6 oz.) custard cups.

2. Beat eggs, pumpkin, milk, sugar, spice and vanilla extract. Carefully pour pumpkin mixture into custard cups.

3. Pour water into pot. Place rack into pot. Place custard cups on rack (water should cover about ¼ of the bottom of the custard cups).

4. Set oven to steam setting for 45 minutes. Cover and cook until custards are just set.

5. Remove custard cups from pot. Let flans cool in cups in cooling rack for 5 minutes. Cover custard cups and refrigerate at least 4 hours.

6. Loosen edges of flans with a knife. Invert onto dessert plates the serve.

Maple Syrup & Walnut Cake

Preparation time: 20 minutes

Cooking time: 40 minutes

Total time: 60 minutes

Serves: 1 to 3 people

Recipe Ingredients:

- 1 cup of pure maple syrup
- 1 cup of sour cream
- 30g of unsalted butter, melted
- 1 tsp. of pure vanilla extract
- 1 large egg
- 2½ cups of all-purpose/plain flour
- 1 level tsp. of baking soda (also known as bicarb soda)
- ½ cup of toasted walnuts, roughly chopped
- ½ tsp. of salt (We left out the salt)

Cooking Instructions:

1. Mix all ingredients together. Spray baking pan lightly with Pam and pour in pan.

2. Set Ninja to Oven mode and bake on oven setting of 350°F for 50 minutes. Set the pan down in the Ninja on the pyramid mat.

3. Serve and enjoy.

Old fashioned Rice Pudding

Preparation time: 10 minutes

Cooking time: 60 minutes

Total time: 60 minutes Serves:

1 to 3 people

Recipe Ingredients:

- 2 cups of instant rice
- 2 cups of milk
- ½ cup of sugar
- 1 tbsp. of butter
- ½ tsp. of salt
- 1 tsp. of vanilla
- ½ tsp. of nutmeg

Cooking Instructions:

1. Combine all ingredients together, put into a buttered quart baking dish. Place the baking dish on the rack.

2. Set Ninja to oven mode and bake at 350°F for 1 hour. Stirring after 15 minutes and again when pudding is done.

3. Taste to see if you need to stir in more of nutmeg or sugar. Sprinkle a little cinnamon on the top. Pudding will thicken as it cools.

4. Serve it hot or chilled.

Scalloped Pineapple

Preparation time: 30 minutes

Cooking time: 1 hour 30 minutes

Gross time: 2 hours

Serves: 4 to 8 people

Recipe Ingredients:

- 4 cups of bread crumbs (no crusts)
- 1 stick of melted butter
- ½ cup of milk
- 1 cup of sugar
- 20 ounces of can of crushed pineapple (do not drain)

Cooking Instructions:

1. Add all ingredients as listed to your Ninja and set Ninja to Slow Cook mode and cook at Low pressure for 2 hours.

2. After 2 hours, serve and enjoy.

Yogurt Cake

Preparation time: 10 minutes

Cooking time: 50 minutes

Gross time: 60 minutes

Serves: 4 to 6 people

Recipe Ingredients:

- 1 cup of Greek Yogurt unflavoured (we used Non-Fat)
- 1 cup of water
- 1 greased Ninja Pan (we used pam baking spray)

Cooking Instructions:

1. Turn your Ninja to Oven setting and allow Ninja to preheat for 15 minutes at 350°F degrees.

2. In a medium mixing bowl, mix ingredients for about two minutes. Put into greased Ninja Pan.

3. Now set Ninja to Oven mode and bake for about 60 to 65 minutes at 350°F degrees. Check with toothpick.

4. Serve with powdered sugar sprinkled and Cool Whip or icing. Delicious!

Acknowledgement

In preparing the "Foodi Multi-Cooker Cookbook Beginners", I sincerely wish to acknowledge my indebtedness to my husband for his support and the wholehearted cooperation and vast experience of my two colleagues - Mrs. Alexandra Bedria, and Mrs. Barbara miles.

REBECCA PACE